D0306316

The following Motley Fool books are also published by Boxtree:

The Motley Fool UK Investment Guide (2nd edition)
The Motley Fool UK Investment Workbook
The Fool's Guide to Investment Clubs
The Fool's Guide to Online Investing
How to Invest When You Don't Have Any Money: The Fool's Guide
The Motley Fool's Rule Breakers, Rule Makers
The Old Fool's Retirement Guide (available November 2000)

Make Your Child
a Millionaire:
The Fool's Guide

Alan Oscroft

BOXTREE

First published 2000 by Boxtree
an imprint of Macmillan Publishers Ltd
25 Eccleston Place, London SW1W 9NF
Basingstoke and Oxford

www.macmillan.co.uk

Associated companies throughout the world

ISBN 0 7522 7173 3

9 8 7 6 5 4 3

A CIP catalogue record for this book is available from
the British Library.

Typeset by SX Composing DTP, Rayleigh, Essex
Printed in Great Britain by Mackays of Chatham plc, Kent

Extract from 'The Parent' by Ogden Nash used by kind
permission of Andre Deutsch Ltd.

Contents

Foreword:
In the Beginning,
There was a Title . . .

Without any further ado, here and now, let's acknowledge that *Make Your Child a Millionaire* was conceived as an eye-catching title. It was designed to jerk you out of that glazed stupor induced by endless ranks of bookshop shelves crammed with every title under the sun, and to cause you to expostulate in the following fashion: 'Why, that fine title seems just the ticket! I shall pluck it from its display position, flick at random through several of its pages and purchase same from the spotty fellow at the till.'

The thing about eye-catching titles, though, is that eventually they have to deliver. It would be no good seducing you with a natty title and then failing to come up with the goods. In business parlance, we'd have passed the customer acquisition test, but failed roundly on the customer retention side of things. And as any business person will tell you, that is No Good At All.

Ultimately, you'll be the judge of whether this book delivers or not. If you're interested in my opinion, then I think it does, and handsomely so. I'd like to say that this is because of how Alan Oscroft has taken extraordinarily complex concepts, previously understandable only to those with a degree in particle physics or similar, and rendered them in language the layman can understand, while at the same time maintaining an engaging, light-hearted and eminently readable style.

I'd like to say this because it would reflect well on Alan, who is a great chap and one of the stalwarts of the Fool in the UK. Unfortunately, I can't, because it's wrong. What Alan has actually done is take extraordinarily simple concepts, understandable only to those with British Association of Gymnastics Award Level 4 or above (the one where you have to do a forward roll), and render them in language the layman can understand, while at the same time maintaining an engaging, light-hearted and eminently readable style.

Don't think I'm downplaying what Alan has done, though. It can be as hard to portray simple concepts as complex ones, and the fact that much of what he is writing about will probably be news to many people is evidence of that. None of us learn much about money or investing at school, from our parents, or anywhere else. This book is designed to help address this very sorry state of affairs. Not only will it help you start to amass a sizeable next egg for that ongoing stake in the genetic lottery you lovingly refer to as your 'children', but it will help you set about endowing them with the skills they need to be responsible for their own financial futures. In the process, it may teach them a thing or two about life. One of the most important things to learn about money, early on, is that you need to approach it with the right attitude. Most of us enter adult life scared of it, its servant rather than its master. That's wrong.

But enough about the content of the book. I'm really here to tell you about Alan and the Motley Fool, not necessarily in that order. I'll start with the Fool, because then I can cunningly interweave the tale of how we found Alan.

The Fool, the Fool! It's a child of the Internet age and could not have existed in any previous communications era. Fools, of course, have always existed. The job of the Fool in the Middle Ages was to poke fun at those in authority, to use the medium of humour and light-hearted banter to depict the world the way it really was, and still come away with their head attached to their shoulders.

It was in this spirit that David and Tom Gardner, two American brothers, founded the Motley Fool in 1993. Much was wrong with the financial establishment in the United States and it had long been evident that most of the financial services industry was concerned with servicing itself rather than its customers. The time was ripe for a few Fools to jump into the picture and start to point out that the Emperor, in fact, was wearing no clothes. But not only did they want to highlight the pernicious practices of the financial services industry, they also wanted to bring out positive messages about the importance of adopting a long-term approach to investing, the power of compounding to increase your wealth and the extraordinary wealth-building effects of holding shares in established, commonly-known companies for extended periods. (Editor's note: extended periods of time are hopefully something children possess even more of than the rest of us.)

The two brothers therefore started a newsletter with their college chum, Erik Rydholm. It was called the *Motley Fool*, its motto was to educate, amuse and enrich and it achieved a circulation of, um, 60.

And there the story would have ended – pretty rapidly, actually – if it hadn't been for the America Online (AOL) service. Using the Internet, this company provided access to its own network, which even at that time had many hundreds of thousands of subscribers and now has over 15 million. Tom Gardner started posting content from the newsletter on the message boards at AOL. All of a sudden, from 60 subscribers, mostly within the Washington DC area, they were getting responses from all over the United States. They had suddenly achieved the distribution of a national newspaper. For free.

So much activity was that they were asked by America Online to host a service, to be called the Motley Fool. Since then the Fool has grown and grown, constantly fuelled by its community of users exchanging ideas and knowledge on the discussion boards. Now, the Fool Web site has around two million visitors a month in the US (**www.fool.com**), a number of bestselling books in print that have sold over a million copies, has its content syndicated across the nation in over 160 newspapers and a nationally syndicated radio show.

It also has an offshoot here in the UK (**www.fool.co.uk**)

which itself has a recently born sibling in Germany (www.fool.de).

The Motley Fool UK was started by myself and Bruce Jackson in 1997. We were both amateur investors and enthusiastic users of the Motley Fool, and were convinced that the Fool had a role in the UK, where there was so much ignorance about financial affairs and where the financial services industry had done anything but distinguish itself in the previous decade. The much-publicized pensions mis-selling scandal is evidence of that, as is the well-known conflict of interest inherent in the kind of commission-based financial advice offered by many so-called 'Independent' Financial Advisers.

Since our founding back then, we have grown from two slightly crazed and very overgrown children working in the evenings from our back rooms (Bruce was a full-time accountant, I was a full-time doctor) to an organization of around 40 full-timers, backed up in many important ways by the resources of the US Fool, which amounts to around another 300 people at the time of writing. In the UK we currently have around 250,000 visitors a month, a number of other books in print besides this one, along with a newspaper column in the *Independent on Sunday* and a number of other content syndications in a variety of media.

Early on in this saga, we came across Alan Oscroft, a software programmer in Bournemouth and a prolific contributor to our discussion boards. It rapidly became apparent that Alan was a star turn and we had to recruit him. Alan briefly mentions a meal at Pizza Express in his acknowledgements. This took place in early summer 1998 – Tom Gardner, one of the co-founders, was in London, so we put out a 'Calling all Fools' pizza invitation on the Web site. We were pretty small then and didn't have many respondents, three in total, in fact, of whom two were Alan and his friend, Yorick. The third was a very smart American, James Kraft, married to an equally smart Liverpudlian, and who had lived in both the UK and

Germany for ten years. He became our Chief Business Fool and is responsible for driving forward the business side of the Motley Fool in Europe. We can safely say that meal was a particularly efficient recruiting effort. We're still working on Yorick. You never know.

Since then, Alan has been bringing his knowledge of money and finance, his eminently Foolish nature, his wit and writing ability to the Fool. The Fool in turn has brought him uncertainty, chaos, insecurity and a relentless sapping of the will to live.

We think the deal's a fair one and happily so does Alan, as he agreed to write this book. So what are his qualifications to do so?

Well, he was a child once.

He is also a terrific communicator and truly passionate about this subject. Honestly, he's usually very mild-mannered, but the lack of financial education in our schools and the aeons of missed opportunity that this represents can make him pretty steamed up. I think some of Alan's passion will communicate itself to you, and that you'll be inspired to set about securing the financial future of the children in your life, and also educating them to think for themselves about money. And of course, thinking for yourself is a habit that's hard to break. By giving young people confidence in one part of their lives - here we happen to be talking about money -- you help them build confidence in other parts too, and this becomes an ever-expanding virtuous circle.

As well as helping you to get the circle turning, this book is a wonderful embodiment of the Fool's triple mission: to educate, amuse and enrich. Of course, as I said earlier, ultimately you must be the judge of that. We hope you'll come back and share your thoughts at the Motley Fool Web site.

David Berger
London
May 2000

Acknowledgements

If I have seen further, it is by standing on the shoulders of giants.
Sir Isaac Newton

It has taken a lot of events to come together for me to end up writing this book, and I would never have guessed, even a short year ago, that I'd be writing a few words here to thank those who have helped. Yes, it's time for a few acknowledgements. I'm not going to go for any of those soppy personal messages that so many people seem to like in these touchy-feely days (you know, stuff like 'thanks for all the love and support' and all that. Yeeuuch!) – no, just a few words to those who helped, and to the people who got me involved with the Motley Fool in the first place.

Thanks first go to Nigel Roberts for lending me his expertise on investing for children, for handling the Motley Fool's Investing for Children discussion board so expertly (and in doing so, providing me with a fair bit of material for this book). Thanks also to him for checking some of my work in search of any blunders (though if any are left by the time you read this, it's my fault, not his, so throw the custard pies at me at some future Motley Fool social get-together if you really want to).

Thanks go to the Foolish triumvirate who were running the UK site when I first discovered it and who organized the now-legendary pizza session at Pizza Express – that's David Berger, Bruce Jackson, and Nigel Roberts. And thanks to Tom Gardner for buying the pizza (oh yeah, and for starting the whole thing up in the first place, with brother David). Extra thanks must also go to David Berger for his persistent attempts to persuade me that I should give up my 20-year career in computer software development, and that life as a full-time

Fool would be much more fun. He was right, it is a lot more fun. It seems so obvious now.

Thanks too to my old mate Yorick (who hates me calling him old) for the copy of the US *Motley Fool Investment Guide* that got me started on all this Fool stuff in the first place, and which Tom G kindly signed for me all that time ago (and no, Yorick, you can't have it back).

Thanks to Stephen Bland and Paul Marshall (better known on the Web as Pyad and JonnyT respectively) for running the Fool's Beat The Footsie and Relative Strength strategies and all their variants, which help to show that ordinary people can prosper on the stock market without any real experience, provided they keep emotions out of it.

Thanks also to James Carlisle for digging out and analyzing the latest Credit Suisse First Boston Equity-Gilt Study, the results of which provide the material for Chapter Four.

Special thanks also go to Peter Hogan, deputy head of Sunderland High School and founder of the school's investment club scheme, for showing me how investing really can be taught at schools in an exciting and meaningful way. And very special thanks go to those pupils (and ex-pupils) at the school who have managed the investment club and who kindly gave up some of their time to talk to me about their experiences. So, Natalie Forster, James Donald, Zoe Marshall, Emily Thomas, Guy McNulty and James Arrowsmith, thanks for helping to make Part 3 of this book a possibility and for proving beyond doubt that young people with no experience, but with the desire to learn and succeed, really can beat the professionals at their own game. Oh, and apologies to Zoe's mum for making her miss her dental appointment.

And last but not least, this list wouldn't be complete without thanking the Ringwood Brewery for providing years of bodily sustenance of a most invigorating kind, and the Porterhouse in Westbourne for serving it up with a smile.

Alan Oscroft

Introduction

Behold the child, by nature's kindly law
Pleased with a rattle, tickled with a straw:
Some livelier plaything gives his youth delight,
A little louder, but as empty quite:
Scarfs, garters, gold, amuse his riper stage,
And beads and prayer-books are the toys of age:
Pleased with this bauble still, as that before;
Till tired he sleeps, and life's poor play is o'er.
Alexander Pope

Apart from personal subsistence (food, clothes, and all that), what do you think is the most expensive thing most people will ever spend their money on over the course of their lifetimes? How about a house? They certainly tend to come with nice big price tickets these days.

Or what about cars? If you buy a new one every two years, particularly if you have expensive tastes, you could easily run up a pretty impressive bill there too.

Holidays! They're costly things too, aren't they? Those fortnights in Clacton-on-Sea (or whatever exotic destination suits your purse and tastes) soon add up. And what if you take an occasional winter skiing break too?

But no!

None of those. You've probably guessed what our answer here is going to be. There's a pretty good chance that for most people, the money spent on raising kids will amount to a fair bit more than keeping the rain out, the wheels turning, and the tan topped up.

According to research carried out a few years ago by the

Joseph Rowntree Foundation, the average child, by the time the little darling reaches the spotty and hormone-laden age of 17, will have cost something in the region of £50,000 in food, clothing and leisure. That is, just the basics. On top of that, you have to buy a bigger house, one with enough bedrooms to fit children in (OK, you'll probably get money back when you sell up and move somewhere smaller later in life, but while the kids are growing up you've got that higher mortgage to cover). You'll need family cars too, and family holidays, and that all adds up. Now add in the loss of one income (even for just the first few years) or add on the cost of child care. Finally, multiply all that expenditure by the number of children you are going to have, and it's going to add up to an awful lot of beer money.

Now, if the amount of money you're going to spend on creating your contribution to the next generation is likely to be rather substantial, then it might be an idea to think seriously about how to place them in the best position to get the most out of the sixty years or thereabouts that they can expect to spend on this planet after they have spread their wings and flown the nest (or have been finally booted out, whichever comes sooner).

And that means putting a bit of cash away for their future years; something to help provide a buffer against hardships, a shelter against life's storms.

'Now wait a minute!' I hear you cry, 'You've just told us how much having children is going to cost, and now you're saying we've got to fork out a whole lot more money to set them up for life.'

But don't panic! Calmly put down the phone and don't make that call to the vasectomy clinic to book your husband's surprise birthday present just yet. Investing a little each month, if it is done sensibly (or 'Foolishly' – and don't forget that capital 'F' – as we like to think of it here at the Motley Fool), won't actually sting you for very much at all. A little invested early makes far more difference than a larger sum invested later on, and time is on your kids' side.

So bear with me as I take a look at why we all need to provide for our old age, and how starting a child off on the right track at a tender age can make a very important difference in later life. That all-important magic, called compound returns, takes time to weave its spell. But if you invest a little, regularly, at a decent rate of return, and over a long enough period, you might be surprised at the size of the sums you can accumulate.

I'll also be taking a wander around the various investment opportunities available for children, how they all compare in the long term, and what legal and regulatory hoops you will have to leap through (though thankfully, there aren't actually too many).

Oh, and we'll say a few words about education too. I learned about the real need to invest myself, and discovered the Foolish way of going about it, rather late in life (just a few years ago, in fact). Making sure your children don't leave it until they're nearly forty to work out that their sixties might not be as comfortable as they had been expecting is one of the best things you can do for them.

But a confession. I'm not speaking from personal experience here, and have spent no time at all changing nappies, warming bottles of milk and all that stuff. Instead, I got myself a ready-made teenage step-daughter when I got married and so have not had the benefits of all those early years of compounding investment returns to help put together her fortune.

Still, it's better late than never. But it's a lot better early than late.

That's enough of that, and here's where you come in. All you have to do now is read the book and then, in the words of Mr Pope, before your own life's poor play is o'er, get out there and start accumulating enough gold for your own children's riper stages.

Alan Oscroft
Liverpool
May 2000

Chapter One: Do you need to bother?

He that hath wife and children, hath given hostages to fortune;
for they are impediments to great enterprises, either of virtue, or
mischief.
Francis Bacon

It doesn't sound as though old man Bacon (and we're talking about the medieval dude here, not the 20th-century painter) was too fond of kids really, and it doesn't sound as though he'd have been too keen on stashing away some of his hard-earned readies to help with their futures. He would probably have approved of this chapter.

Anyway, you've got kids. Or you might be working on having some. Or you may hate the little blighters and have sworn never to have any and you're just reading this book to gloat over the problems that all those suckers who look on parenthood with Utopian naivety will have to face as they sacrifice their young lives to soiled nappies and staying awake all night. Whatever.

If you *do* have kids, their entire lifetimes are going to be your concern, aren't they? Gone are the days, thankfully, when relative poverty forced parents' main ambition for their children to be getting them through school as painlessly as possible, and out into the real world where they could earn a few crusts to contribute to the family income. In the 19th century, it was up a chimney by the age of twelve, over to t'mill (where there was always trouble) when they got too big for the chimneys, and then they were pretty much on their own. That was the lot of many British offspring at the time.

And even in the first half of the century we have just left, most children's expectations were to leave school at 16 and go down the pit, or off to the factories or somewhere equally unattractive, to scrape a living for the rest of their working lives.

It's not quite as bad as that these days though, thanks to the post-war economic boom that the capitalist world has experienced. The 'get the children out to work to contribute some money' philosophy has shifted for a large number of today's families, and new generations are more and more able to guiltlessly provide for their own long-term future without worrying about Mum and Dad going hungry.

In fact, as we enter the 21st century, we are in the middle of a fundamental worldwide shift in family life. For millennia, children were there to look after their parents, and that was a pressing reason for many families to have them in the first place. And in most of the undeveloped and developing world, that is precisely how things still work today. 'If we don't have any children, who'll look after us when we're old?' is still a fundamental question for a large majority of the world's population.

For many families in developed countries (aka free-market capitalist countries) the 'reproduction' focus has actually turned around 180 degrees. Instead of those early years being frustratingly occupied with trying to make ends meet for the family, many of us are becoming more and more able to shift some resources in the direction of our kids' long-term security. We've always wanted our children to have a better life than we had, to enjoy greater wealth, and to see more of the world. But it's only in the last few decades that such an ideal has become practical for more than a privileged few, and that we can help satisfy higher levels of human needs for our kids than those of mere subsistence (see the section below, 'Human Needs'). But is it really necessary? If everything is so much better now, surely they can look after themselves, can't they?

Human needs

The millennia-long development of human society has been pretty much synonymous with the desire to satisfy ever higher levels of human needs, and in 1970 a chap by the name of AH Maslow suggested that human needs fall into a hierarchy of five categories, namely:

- *Physiological needs – food, drink, shelter*
- *Safety needs – protection against danger, threats and deprivation*
- *Social needs – friendship, belonging, acceptance*
- *'Ego' needs – self-esteem, reputation, status*
- *'Self-actualization' needs – self-development and the realization of personal potential.*

He saw it as a hierarchy because the higher levels cannot be reached, and aren't even important in fact, until the lower levels have been satisfied.

For most of human history, the only thing that mattered was survival; individual families couldn't afford to have ambitions beyond keeping their bellies filled, their bodies clothed, the rain and wind at bay, and enemies away. So a large part of it has only been concerned with the satisfaction of the first three levels, though some degree of 'ego-based' need will certainly have entered the picture pretty early on.

The world's most developed societies have thankfully passed this stage, and opportunities for satisfying the highest level of needs are becoming accessible to more and more people. Unfortunately though, many societies are currently stuck somewhere around the 'social needs'/'ego needs' boundary, and are embroiled in the divisions and conflicts that are generated by the resulting urges for tribal domination.

On a happier note, Maslow's approach does suggest that the more that self-actualization needs are satisfied for individuals, the further societies will progress from their days of division and tribal conflict. And that can't be a bad thing, can it?

The key social factor that facilitates the progression of individuals up the hierarchy is wealth. The means of generating that wealth, denied to many for so long, is becoming more and more accessible by ordinary members of society every day. And that, fortunately, is what the Motley Fool is all about.

Here in the UK, when today's forty-somethings (your author, for example) and fifty-somethings were born all those years ago, things were rather simple and most people's lives were planned in a pretty similar way. Well, actually, most people's lives weren't planned at all, they just panned out along the same lines because, well, that's just the way things were and it was just what you did.

A boy born then, in those baby boomer years, would spend 16 years at school, get a job, work until the age of 65, and then retire and live out what was left of his three-score years and ten subsisting on a state pension. A girl would follow a similar path until she got married and had her first child. Then she'd stop work for a couple of decades or so to bring up the kids, perhaps returning to work after they had grown up and putting in another ten or fifteen years before hanging up her work boots at the age of 60.

That was most people, anyway. A minority remained at school for a further two years in search of those precious A-levels that would hopefully provide the passport to a more flexible and profitable career path. And of those few, a smaller number went on to university. But it all came back to the same thing in the end; most of them ended up in full-time employment with the expectation of working out their years, eventually retiring to spend their remaining days watching *Wheel of Fortune* and *Supermarket Sweep* (or whatever it was they did in those barren days before daytime TV).

Old age

Of course, everyone knew that this ideal would lead to a nation of contented old couples living comfortably on their state pensions which, being easily covered by the National Insurance contributions of each subsequent generation of workers, would grow as the nation's wealth grew. That would lead to an equitable distribution of the new wealth that was relentlessly being created by the capitalist miracle, and being directed by the new post-war Socialism.

One of the benefits of living in a position of such relative privilege, surely, is that we don't need to worry too much about our kids' long-term welfare. They're not going to go hungry, any more than we are. And while they're young, you're going to be far more concerned about that letter from the school doctor who's been conducting his latest head lice big game hunt, or about finding the money to pay for that 'educational' skiing trip that 'everyone else is going on and I just have to go with them if I don't want be left out' than you are about providing for the little darlings' later years, aren't you? After all, it'll be a good few decades yet before they'll need to buy those nice zip-up slippers and the cat will need its daily ration of *Pussy Chunks*. And there'll be a state pension for them, just like the one you're going to get yourself, and it will have kept pace with the cost of living, won't it? And then there'll be occupational pension schemes and personal pensions and all the rest. Anyway, you'll be pushing up the daisies by the time it matters, so it's not your worry.

And even if you think you really do need to do something about your descendents' family fortune, there's hardly anything that you *can* do with the tiny amount of money left over from the monthly spending on disposable nappies (or 'landfill', as they are known in some circles), hypo-allergenic washing powder, and dozens of tins of *Kiddie-Scoff*, is there? What possible difference could that modest amount make over the long term, when compared to the vastly superior earning power that your bouncing offspring are going to have in twenty years' time?

Education

So you don't need to worry about the children's old age, but what about their educational needs?

That's all handled by the state machinery too, isn't it? We Brits are in the very enviable position of enjoying 'free' education up until the age of eighteen, aren't we? And we don't have to contribute a single penny outside our Tax and National Insurance contributions.

But just supposing that little Boris or Doris turns out to be quite smart and that some sort of further education might be in order. How does that work these days, and who pays for it? A lot of us can remember the university grant system, by which many an aspiring young Einstein or Descartes' earthly needs were taken care of by a thrice-yearly stipend from the Government, leaving them free to attend to more cerebral matters without worrying about their next pangs of hunger (or, in some people's view, the Government paid the bar bills and left the students to handle the hangovers; the author, an ex-student, declines to comment).

OK, we know that those great old grant days are behind us, and that advanced scholastic funding comes in the form of loans these days. But that's not too bad, is it? The interest rate is rather good, and most grown-ups would love to be able to borrow money so cheaply. It's a good education in itself too, and helps prepare students for the realities of managing their personal finances in later years, don't you think? And it's only fair. With more and more people aspiring to further education these days (and being in a comfortable enough position not to have to rush out and look for any job they can find as soon as they leave school), isn't it better to distribute the available money more thinly to a greater number of people?

So, we know our kids' pension years will be taken care of and their old-age supply of tea bags should be pretty secure, and we now also know that we don't need to worry too much about their education. They'll get a decent enough state education until adulthood, and then the means (albeit fairly limited) to go on further if they need it.

Yes, quite.

Health
What about health? There's another thing that people need to worry about when they get older. Older bodies mean more aches and pains and more illnesses that need to be taken care of. But again, we really don't need to be concerned, do we? The National Health Service will always be going strong, and nobody will ever have to worry about private medicine or paying for health insurance if they really don't want to, will they? No, surely not; perish the thought!

All roses?
Remember the post-war Socialist dream that we mentioned a few paragraphs ago? How close to that dream does reality actually approach? It's true that a lot of things have changed since the days of those old family- and gender-based role-playing ideals (which many more enlightened people never cared for much anyway). Many of them have changed for the better, providing great advances in personal freedom and the breakdown of gender stereotyping.

But many of those early and somewhat naive visions of personal financial security are being eroded. Do you really believe that comfortable pensions for all will be a reality in the second half of this century? Or that education and health for all will be guaranteed? If you do, you should perhaps close the book, put your rose-tinted spectacles back on, and relax into a life of confident delusion.

But if you think that the future will be filled with uncertainty, and that the only way for individuals to assure themselves of a reasonable level of comfort throughout their lives will be by taking control for themselves and planning their own futures, from as young an age as possible, then we're right with you.

Read on.

Chapter Two: Yes, you do need to bother

How pleasant it is to have money, hey ho! How pleasant it is to have money.
Arthur Hugh Clough

Even if you're not convinced that you need to bother about the financial viability of your family line, you might just be harbouring the suspicion that we think a little differently at the Motley Fool. In fact, if we didn't, this would be a pretty thin book, and it would have stopped at the first chapter. The presence of all those pages in your hand rather gives the game away.

In the previous chapter we looked at the ideal world envisaged by Aneurin Bevan and his enlightened friends and colleagues, who dreamed up the Welfare State back in the 1940s. We are now going to re-examine it, but from a slightly more critical standpoint. But before we do, we'd like to make one thing clear: we do not mean to disparage the good Mr Bevan and his noble aims. In fact, a Foolish cap is humbly doffed to him in the hope that somewhere his spirit can hear the jangling of its Foolish bells. We think (well, the author thinks, anyway) that the Welfare State, with its provision of some sort of social security, and the development of the National Health Service, were pretty good things that came along at a critical time. They are indeed the envy of many a developing nation, but they are imperfect and are likely to become less and less appropriate as times change.

Though the Welfare State has provided a welcome safety net for several generations, its main provision for long-term financial security is seriously flawed and is just not going to provide future generations with the kind of secure income that many people might think. We are talking, of course, about the state pension system.

The State Pension system
The state pension system consists of two parts, the Basic Pension and the State Earnings Related Pension Scheme (or SERPS, as it is known).

Basic pension
The basic pension currently stands at a handsome £67.50 per week for a single person, and for a married couple it comes in at a majestic £107.90. If both partners are entitled to a single person pension, and these total more than £107.90, then they get the two single pensions instead. The basic pension is increased annually with inflation. Not everybody qualifies for the basic pension, though; you need to have made a minimum level of National Insurance contributions to qualify. Roughly speaking, if you've earned at least the same amount as the basic pension for most of your working life then you should be OK.

SERPS and contracting out
The basic pension is designed to replace your lowest slice of income (that is, up to £67.50 per week). The next part, the State Earnings Related Pension Scheme (SERPS) replaces the next slice of your income – the section between £67.50 and £500 per week. It is 'earnings-related' because the more you earn (below £500), the more you get. However, as you move from £67.50 to £500, a lower and lower percentage of your income is actually replaced. This means that someone earning, say, £200 per week will retire on a higher percentage of their pre-retirement income than someone who was earning £500 per week (although they will, of

*course, get less actual money). Income above the £500 per week
level does not get replaced under SERPS. SERPS is also only
available for employees, not the self-employed.*

*If you want, you can choose to opt out of SERPS. This is called
'contracting out'. The effect of this is that your National Insurance
payments, which would have gone towards providing your SERPS
benefits, instead get paid into your occupational or personal
pension. Your pension scheme then guarantees to pay out at least
the SERPS benefits that you have given up. Basically, all you are
doing is replacing SERPS with your own arrangements.*

*Note that you can only contract out of SERPS. You cannot
contract out of the basic state pension.*

The state pension scheme looks to be pretty reasonable at first
glance, doesn't it? OK, you might not think that the basic
pension will buy very much, but it's not a bad start and SERPS
will take care of the rest, surely. But the basic pension portion
has changed in one very significant detail since its conception,
and the very good reason for it is that Britain's demographics,
that is the make-up of our society, has changed quite a bit in
the last fifty years and is still changing. Before we examine the
change itself, let's see how that pension is paid for.

When it was first thought up, the funding of the state
pension was pretty simple: the National Insurance contributions of people in work paid the pensions of those who had
retired. And it worked just fine. In 1948, there were approximately 5.5 million people in the UK over the age of 65, a figure
which represented 10.7 per cent of the population.

Back then, the proportion of people in work was high
relative to the proportion of the population who had retired,
and sufficient National Insurance contributions were coming
in to meet the demand for pension cash. But in some ways, the
Welfare State system has since been a victim of its own success.
As the National Health system brought decent health care to
all, and as the pace of medical advances increased, people
began to live longer, and to enjoy much improved health and

more active lifestyles in their old age. And this means that today, the proportion of the population over retirement age has increased significantly, with the percentage of the population in work falling as a result.

In fact, by 1997 the number of people over the age of 65 had grown to 9.3 million, representing 15.7 per cent of the population. That means an increase of nearly 50 per cent in the over-65 portion of the population, and a similar proportional increase in the cost of pensions. And in the future, the problem is going to get worse, with some estimates suggesting that people over the age of 65 will make up as much as 23 per cent of the population by 2031. And that's going to cost an awful lot in pension cash.

So, things don't look quite so healthy now (so to speak) as they did in 1948, do they? When the pension system was set up, the basic pension portion was geared to average earnings and increased in line with them. But for this to be sustainable, the number of people in work would have to stay in proportion to the number of people drawing their pension. But that's not what has happened, and something had to break. Either our National Insurance contributions would have to rise, or the value of the basic pension would have to fall. It was, in fact, the latter that happened, when the Conservative government of Margaret Thatcher broke the link with average earnings, gearing pension payments to inflation instead.

Now that was a very clever thing to do (and whatever you think of old Maggie, she was generally a pretty shrewd politician). And that's because, with average earnings growing at just a couple of percentage points above inflation, most people didn't seem to think the change really made much difference. A public uproar was not heard, and pension riots were not seen in central London the way poll tax riots were (oh yes, the poll tax riots; maybe she wasn't *that* shrewd all the time).

But if you work it out, you might be surprised at just how much difference a couple of percentage points can make over the long term.

Just a couple of per cent

Here's a question for you; a little something to tax those grey cells and see how alert you are. Suppose two little tykes are lucky enough to have parents who start saving a little money every month, say £25, month in, month out, never missing a month. They do this until our little heroes aren't so little any more and reach the age of 21. The money is then cashed in and handed over to each of them as a surprise 21st birthday present. Now, most 21-year-olds that we know would blow a fair bit of that money on a hangover, but these two have been educated the Fool way and they decide to leave the money where it is, and continue to make those £25 per month contributions themselves until they reach the age of 60.

Let's suppose that baby Fred's parents save the money in a building society account that achieves an average return of 6 per cent per year over the 60 years. The other two, little Wilma's parents, put the money into a stock market fund that isn't great, but manages 8 per cent per year over the same period.

When the 60 years are up, how much difference will those two percentage points make? We're going to make it a bit easier on you by making this a multiple-choice question, and if you don't get the answer right, don't worry, you will be in good company; most people would get it wrong (and we haven't even told you how to work it out yet, but we will later if you're very good).

At the end of 60 years, Fred will have amassed £165,000.

Question 1) How much will Wilma have, approximately, with a return that is just two percentage points better per year than Fred's?

a) £190,000
b) £252,000
c) £392,000
d) £15,000,000

The possibly surprising correct answer is c. Wilma will be sitting on £392,000, which is nearly two and a half times Fred's wealth (and if you went for option d, hey, come on, be serious. This is a book about investing, not a fairy tale).

But of course, you'll do better for your kids, won't you? What if you and your sprog manage a return of 10 per cent per year over 60 years? Next question. . .

Question 2) With a return of 10 per cent per year, how much will your kid retire on aged 60?

a) £623,000
b) £884,000
c) £959,000

The answer is c – £959,000. There, you're hardly into the book and you already know how to make your kid a millionaire. Well, nearly. So here's your second chance to put the book down and switch on the telly. Or, if you want, you can read on and find out what your kid might really be worth some day.

We'll talk a lot more about compound returns soon, but for now let's introduce the Fool's Rules for Kids numbers 1 and 2.

Rule 1)   Small differences in returns matter. A lot.
Rule 2)   Never forget Rule 1.

If the basic state pension grows at the same rate as inflation, instead of at the same rate as average earnings, and assuming that earnings growth continues to beat inflation over the years (which is what happens in an expanding economy, as it represents the creation of genuine new wealth), retired folk of the future will be able to buy the same amount of bread, tea, baked beans, holidays, computers or whatever as today's pensioners. Does that sound sufficient? Superficially, it might.

But over the same period, people in work will be able to buy more and more of the same stuff each year, as their real wealth (that is, the growth in their retained earnings after allowing for inflation) increases. And they'll be able to buy newer, more expensive, things as they come along too. Over the years, pensioners will become relatively less wealthy than those in work (and remember the gap in earnings made by those two teeny weeny percentage points over the long term), and people newly retiring will suffer a much bigger drop in income when they retire then people retiring today. And Fred and Wilma? The pensioners will be the Freds and the workers the Wilmas.

Doesn't sound so good when you think of it like that, does it? It really is a wonder we didn't see pensions riots in the City.

Company Pensions and Personal Pensions

We might also have thought that company pensions and personal pensions would provide enough cash for a comfortable old age. A company pension can be a good thing to have, particularly if the company is providing a generous contribution, but a typical company pension is likely to offer you something like two-thirds of your final salary. Not bad, perhaps, but the combination of longer leisure hours and less money to spend is not going to result in a better lifestyle. If they want to spend those extra hours doing lots of fun things, your kids will most likely need more than a company pension to support themselves.

We've heard a lot about personal pensions in recent years, mostly as a result of the lamentable personal pensions mis-selling scandal. Pension companies went to all sorts of lengths to persuade individuals to opt out of the SERPS portion of their state pension, or to opt out of company pensions, and put their contributions into personal pension plans instead. The problem was that in many cases it was not done honestly and transparently, and people ended up with pension plans that simply were not going to provide them with as much money as their prior arrangements would have done. The aim of the guilty pensions companies was to maximize their own commissions, not to improve their customers' pension arrangements. Scandalous; but at least we have seen some redress recently.

Although personal pension contributions enjoy a tax break, a large portion of that tax break actually ends up going into the pockets of the pension providers due to their high charges and their long-term poor performance. When you retire, legislation currently forces you to invest the accumulated cash in an annuity (you can hold this off for a while, but you'll have to buy one by the time you reach 75, or 80 under the latest proposed rule change). An annuity is a financial product that is bought from an investment company, which provides you with a guaranteed annual income. Sounds fair? Wait a minute. The annual rate of return on your capital is actually pretty low, not much better than a building society account, and you have to sacrifice your capital into the bargain. Yes, that's right, the investment company keeps all your capital and gives none of it back to your estate if you die young.

Is that the kind of deal that you want for your children when they retire, or would you prefer to think of them getting a better rate of return and hanging on to their capital to spend as they please, or to pass on to their own offspring if they so desire?

Education

We pondered education briefly in the last chapter too, and it's all free, isn't it? No, it isn't all free, and higher education is getting less free each year. Higher education used to be funded by grants some years ago, but these have slowly but surely been replaced by student loans. Many graduates leave university or college with significant debts these days. Student loans are relatively cheap, but do you really want your children starting out on their own careers with debt hanging around their necks before they've even earned their first penny?

In the future, education is surely going to become more expensive, not cheaper. The main reason for this is that if current trends are anything to go by, more and more people are going to take the opportunities to partake in higher education. But there won't be a steadily increasing amount of money appearing as if by magic to pay for it, and the contents of the education pot will end up being spread more and more thinly. If more people are to have a chance, the amount of cash dished out per individual will have to fall, which actually seems to be quite an equitable way of going about it.

So some money might be needed for higher education too.

And who knows, you might feel that your children's earlier educational needs won't be best suited by the local comprehensive school, and you might be considering private education in one form or another.

Health

National Health waiting lists. They're not so good, are they? Whatever your personal political or moral opinions regarding the relative merits of the National Health Service as against private health care, one thing is certain: private health care is here to stay, and is going to become increasingly popular. As individual wealth increases, it brings with it extra opportunities for choice when it comes to health treatment. For more and more people, the options of choosing alternative therapies, private doctors with no waiting lists, or more expensive drugs that their National Health doctors are not allowed to prescribe, are becoming a reality. Do you want your kids to be left out?

You might well have a moral objection to private health care, but if it came to a choice between spending money to get what you considered to be the best for your child or leaving him or her on a long waiting list or at the mercy of cheaper conventional treatment, which would you prefer?

Investing for their futures doesn't force your children to use private health care, but it will help to give them the choice.

Money, money, money

If none of this has convinced you that putting aside a little money for your children's rainy days (and maximizing the long-term returns they're going to get from it too, of course) is a good idea, then let's think about one last thing.

We Brits are a pretty reserved bunch really, and we don't like talking about money. Oh no, it's a taboo subject that we're not supposed to bring up in polite company. But when it is raised, it is one of the most common subjects of gossip the country over. . .

'Ooh, her at number 11, she's been having problems, I hear.'

'Yes, she's had it all taken away, you know.'

'She hasn't, has she? When did that happen?'

'Well, let me think, it was last Thursday I think. Yes, that's right'

'Never, what happened?'

They came in the morning. Took it all they did, telly, fridge, furniture, the lot. Couldn't keep up the payments, you see.'

Isn't it strange the way financial misfortune seems to be such a popular topic of conversation, while the successful accumulation of personal wealth is seen as such a vulgar one? But ask yourself one question. . .

What, exactly, is wrong with money?

And why shouldn't we try to maximize the amount of the stuff we have?

OK, that's two questions, but it's hard to think of any decent answers to them, isn't it?

Now, at the Motley Fool, we certainly don't advocate putting the pursuit of wealth above all other endeavours. No, money is a means to an end, and that end is the maximization of personal satisfaction.

A Fool's guide to personal satisfaction

Just what is personal satisfaction, and how do you measure it? If you asked a hundred people, you'd probably get two hundred different answers. To some it is measured in material possessions – whoever dies with the most toys wins. To others it means intellectual or spiritual fulfilment (or both). Some people get their satisfaction by striving for artistic or moral achievements. Others devote their lives to charitable causes. Still others see improved political freedom and human rights as their aim in life. And to some, satisfaction is measured by how much their head hurts the next morning.

To most people though, personal satisfaction is derived from a combination of some, or all, the things mentioned above (and other things not mentioned, of course). But whatever it means to you, you want it to be maximized, don't you? At its most simple level, the pursuit of personal satisfaction goes as follows:

Step 1)   Is personal satisfaction maximized?
Step 2)   If yes, go to Step 6.
Step 3)   If no, go to Step 4.
Step 4)   Increase personal satisfaction.
Step 5)   Go to Step 1.
Step 6)   You're there!

Step 4 is the tricky bit. But stop for a moment and think about what personal satisfaction means to you, and think about what it might mean to your children over the course of their lives. Now ask yourself the following question.

Will having a bit more money make Step 4 any easier?

Bit of an easy question, isn't it? There won't be very many people who can honestly answer 'No' to that for themselves, though there will certainly be some. But when it comes to our children, not a single person can honestly answer 'No', for the simple reason that we just don't know what their personal goals and ambitions are going to be over their lifetimes. Valid answers might include, 'Almost Certainly', or 'Probably', or at worst, 'I don't know'.

Our American cousins are a fair bit less reserved than us when it comes to making, investing, spending, and generally shouting about money. If we try to think American for a moment (and I hope not too many of you cringe at the prospect) and look at our good old British foibles from more of a distance, we might just see that there's something to this money lark, and it just might be a nice thing to have loads of.

Now, you don't have to go out and change your bowler for a stetson (or turn your baseball cap round to point backwards). But it might be nice for a smidgen of American comfort with the subject of money to find its way into British psychology, don't you think? So try thinking positively about making, investing and spending money. And you really don't have to shout about it too much if you don't want to.

But where is all this leading, in its long-winded fashion? One last question for you.

Would you like your children to spend their lives. . .

a) Strapped for cash?
b) Scraping by?
c) Reasonably comfortably?
d) Rolling in it?

You'll probably answer c or d. But go on, be a devil, go all the way and plump for d. If you can think of no other reason for investing for your children, then remember the opening words from Arthur Hugh Clough at the beginning of the chapter, and do it just to try and launch them on their voyage to adulthood with more freedom and choice than you ever had. The chances are they'll love you for it, especially if you've educated them to understand money and how to use it well.

You might be surprised to find that your chances of achieving this noble aim are a lot higher than you always thought.

Chapter Three: Time is on their side

And pluck till time and times are done
The silver apples of the moon,
The golden apples of the sun.
W.B. Yeats

If time really is money, then to make serious money from investment you need a serious amount of time. You might get lucky and make some big killings in a short space of time, but very few people are capable of doing that, and even fewer can do it repeatedly. There are no reliable recipes for short-term wealth creation either, so don't put any faith in gurus who try to tell you that they, and only they, have found the secret to Getting Rich Quick. And we're using capital letters here, because Getting Rich Quick is a very important concept for Fools.

'Surely not!' you may gasp, but it really is important and here's why – Getting Rich Quick is probably the single most dangerous thing that you can try to do with your money, and thousands of investors over the ages have ended up losing everything instead. From investing in stock in the South Seas company, to mortgaging the house to buy Dutch tulip bulbs; from buying shares in the highly-geared investment trusts of 1929, to putting it all into unaccountable ostrich farming schemes, to jumping on any popular bandwagon that comes along – we've seen all the tricks in the book, and they all come to naught.

Why is it that otherwise rational people, who will sensibly shop around to save a few pounds on their weekly shopping bill or a few hundred when they buy a new car, will at the same time gamble all their savings on the latest investment craze? The reason is as old as the human race: Envy and Greed, pure and simple (and those words are capitalized too, because they are also things to be studiously avoided). We become envious when we see people all around us raking in the cash from the latest investment bandwagon, and our greed makes us want to get in on it so badly that we throw our otherwise sober and rational judgement to the wind and jump aboard. But when it's crowded, and there are no more left to jump aboard, and we want to get off. . . Well, we know the result.

We've all heard the hackneyed old maxim, 'If it sounds like it's too good to be true, it isn't true.' Why do people keep saying it? Because it's true, that's why. It always has been and always will be, and if you remember just one single investment guideline, then that one wouldn't be such a bad one to go for.

OK, so you keep hearing the Motley Fool going on about long-term investing and how it takes time to get yourself some serious low-risk riches. And you must be wondering when we're going to get on to that recipe for long-term investing. Well, it has two simple ingredients. All you need is a reasonable rate of return (the stratospheric gains that we've been hearing about from some Internet start-up companies when they first float aren't needed, just something approaching the long-term stock market average will be perfectly adequate). And you need some time. Stir them together and sit back, allow them to simmer for a few decades, and you'll be laughing.

Decades! When you've already got a few decades under your belt, thinking that you are going to need a few more if you want to turn your modest monthly savings into a reasonable sum might not fill you with excitement. But young children have decades at their disposal and you can help them make the most of them.

How does all this magic work, then?

Before we attempt to answer that, you might be interested

in taking a look at this section, 'The chessboard question'. Go ahead. We'll wait for you at the other end.

The chessboard question

Here's a little puzzle for you to keep at the back of your mind while you're reading this chapter and unravelling the wonders that time will weave on your savings, given half a chance.

You must have heard the old story about the lad who did some favour or other for a King and, when offered a reward, turned down gold and jewels and asked instead for a single grain of rice to be placed on the first square of a chessboard. Then two grains on the second square, four on the next and so on, doubling up the number of grains for each square until all 64 squares were occupied.

The story ends with the old King agreeing, only to be told that he actually owes the lad rather a lot of rice. Unfortunately though, the storyteller never bothers to work out the final total. And that's where you come in.

Most people don't actually go around investing rice, of course, and it isn't much good as a currency anyway (imagine how many boxes of Uncle Ben's you'd need to put down as deposit on a house), so we'll use pennies instead. Now, suppose some kindly (and wealthy) benefactor offered to provide you with a considerable fortune, and all you had to do was choose which one of the following three options you would like...

1) £250 million.

2) The equivalent of £100 a month invested for 60 years at 20 per cent interest per year.

3) A penny on the first square of a chessboard, doubled up for each subsequent square.

So which one is it? We'll come back with the answer at the end of the chapter.

OK, back to the magic spell. It works through something called 'compounding of returns'. Answer this question: if you invest £100 in year one at an interest rate of 10 per cent, how much have you got after two years? Intuitively, a lot of people would say £120, because 10 per cent of £100 is £10 and you get two years' worth of that. But it's better. Sure, you get your £10 interest after one year, giving a total of £110. But the second year you get 10 per cent of £110, not 10 per cent of £100. So after two years you've got £121, not £120. 'So what, what's a pound between friends?' you might ask. Tut! Tut! Have you already forgotten little Wilma and Fred from the last chapter, and how much their moderate investments turned into?

Working out compound returns for £100 at 10 per cent over two years is pretty easy, and you can do it year by year without too much sweat. But how much money will you end up with after 19 years if you start by investing a lump sum of £833 and add £27 per month thereafter? 'Hmm,' we hear you think, 'you're beginning to sound like my old schoolteacher, who made this stuff about as exciting as washing socks'. And you're right, there must surely be an easier way to go about it.

In fact, there are two ways you could use to work it out, which we will come to in due course, but the great thing is that you don't actually need to be able to work out any of this stuff to be a good investor. You don't need to calculate the actual difference in returns between one investment at 9 per cent and another at 11.5 per cent, for example; all you need is to be able to appreciate the vast difference it can make, given a long enough period. When you have really grasped that, and have understood how much money you stand to lose by settling for even slightly inferior rates of return, you might want to slap yourself on the forehead and curse that teacher one more time for not drumming it into you well enough.

Oh, and you might like to make sure your own kids learn it a bit better too, and that's where Appendix A comes in, where we will talk about how to go about it in more detail. But now, on with some more examples, just to show how powerful the magic really is.

The difference a point makes

In the last chapter, we looked at Fred and Wilma and saw the difference that an extra two percentage points on your annual return actually makes. But we only looked at returns of 6 per cent and 8 per cent, and the returns that people obtain in practice vary a lot more than this.

In fact, going by the average historical UK stock market performance from 1869 to the end of 1999, we find annual returns of 9.8 per cent. In case you're wondering, that figure comes from the CSFB Equity-Gilt Study, something you'll read more about shortly. And since the end of the First World War, in 1918, we see average returns coming in at around the 12.2 per cent mark – a figure from another study that we'll soon introduce you to, the Barclays Capital Equity-Gilt Study. So let's expand on that a little and see how five different children will do if their parents manage to achieve annual returns of 6 per cent, 9.8 per cent, 12.2 per cent, 15 per cent and 20 per cent respectively. Assuming the parents all start investing for the kids when they are born, and the kids take over the responsibility themselves at a suitable age, continuing with exactly the same investment returns, here's the amount of dosh that they will each accumulate. . .

AGE	FRED 6%	WILMA 9.8%	BARNEY 12.2%	BETTY 15%	PEBBLES 20%
10	£4,082	£4,983	£5,661	£6,575	£8,608
16	£7,950	£11,156	£13,900	£18,044	£28,995
18	£9,570	£14,112	£18,176	£24,560	£42,483
21	£12,384	£19,724	£26,753	£38,477	£74,617
35	£34,507	£81,721	£144,555	£285,371	£977,656
40	£47,924	£132,341	£259,075	£576,167	£2,435,188
50	£89,906	£342,051	£824,793	£2,337,491	£15,086,651
60	£165,090	£876,177	£2,613,458	£9,463,032	£93,421,176

What do you think of that? Fred's investment wealth at the age of 60, going on a rate of return that is pretty typical (nay, generous) for a bank or building society savings account, will amount to the sum of £165,090. Wilma, this time earning 9.8 per cent (which, you'll remember from just a few lines ago, is the average rate of return from the stock market during the period from 1869 to the end of 1999), is looking at reaching the age of 60 with £876,177 salted away, which is nearly five and a half times Fred's amount. Wow! That is such a difference, it's worth repeating. . .

- *An increase in the rate of return of just 3.8 percentage points can, over 60 years, net you nearly five and a half times as much money.*

But we don't want you to go away with nearly nine hundred thousand pounds, we want you to go away with more. Young Barney does a little bit better and, over his six decades, matches the average return that the UK stock market has achieved since 1918. That's 12.2 per cent, and those extra 2.4 percentage points net him £2,613,458, which is nearly three times as much money as Wilma! So. . .

- *An increase in the rate of return of just 2.4 percentage points can, over 60 years, net you three times as much money.*

If you do manage to achieve a regular return of 12.2 per cent over most of your lifetime, then you will have done pretty well and you can give yourself a pat on the back. (Actually, with that kind of money, you'll be able to have your personal masseur pat your back for you. No, tell you what, bung us a few quid at the Fool and we'll come and do the back-patting ourselves).

But we don't want you to go away with two and a half million quid either. No, we'd love to give you the next cheque up, which is what Betty achieved. And look at the size of that one. If you can make a return of 15 per cent, you'll end up with nine and a half million pounds.

- *An extra 2.8 percentage points over 60 years can give you three and a half times as much money.*

OK, we're getting into minority territory now, and there aren't many investors who have demonstrated the kind of success that makes 15 per cent year in, year out. Not over six decades anyway. Mind you, the Motley Fool has back-tested some mechanical strategies that have, over an admittedly shorter period of just a couple of decades or so, beaten 15 per cent per year quite nicely.

Most people would be rather ecstatic if they reached the age of 60 with nine and a half big ones in the bank, but let's push it one stage further and see what 20 per cent per year will get. It will get you £93,421,176, that's what. If you haven't been staggered by the sums we've been bandying around so far, you certainly should be now. Because. . .

- *The final extra 5 percentage points net you ten times as much money.*

Remember those two Fool's Rules for Kids we introduced in the last chapter? Let's see them again here as a reminder.

Rule 1)   Small differences in returns matter. A lot.

Rule 2)   Never forget Rule 1.

But this compounding will work just as well if you leave your investing until you start working, won't it? And a young adult in employment will be able to invest a lot more money every month than the amount a struggling parent can muster. So why make raising a child more expensive than it needs to be – it isn't going to make *that* much difference when you start, surely?

Oh, but it is. We've seen what a better annual return can do, but what about those extra years?

The difference a year makes

It's back to Fred and Wilma again, but a different scenario now. This time, Fred's parents put the same old £25 a month away for him, just as before. But Wilma's parents don't think that a measly £25 per month is going to make all that much difference. They're convinced that their daughter is going to be a world-beater (don't all parents think the same?) and will be able to invest far more than £25 every month once she's been to university, graduated with her combined honours degree in advanced poultry farming and polar exploration, and gone on to establish a worldwide franchized chain of *Antarctic Fried Penguin* fast-food restaurants.

So Wilma's Mum and Dad, bless 'em, don't put anything away for her later years.

Meanwhile, assuming that Fred's parents average that magic 9.8 per cent annual return that the UK stock market has returned over the past 130 years (from 1869 to 1999), how much will each of our two young subjects have stashed away when they reach the tender age of 21? Come on, you should be able to give us the answer quick as a flash (if you've been paying attention, that is: hint – the answer's in the table above). The situation after 21 years will be. . .

AGE	FRED 9.8%	WILMA 0%
21	£19,724	£0

Not a bad start for Fred, then. But poor old Wilma, eh?

At age 21, Fred turns out to be a bit of a lad. He hasn't taken any notice of all the stuff his parents have taught him over the years about investing for his future and how the magic of compounding returns will fill his pockets to overflowing. And he hasn't even opened any of those Motley Fool books that they bought him in the hope that he'd learn something that way. No, he's clueless about money, so when he starts work he doesn't save a single penny towards providing for himself later in life. And the only reason he doesn't fritter away the investments that his parents have accumulated for him is because they've hidden all the share certificates so that at least something is preserved. But they're damned if they're going to carry on investing for him now that he can look after himself. That's all he's jolly well going to get.

Wilma, on the other hand, doesn't quite make it as the Colonel Sanders of the *Sphenisciforme* world, but she does get a decent job and, being quite the Fool, immediately starts stashing away £100 a month, continuing until she reaches her 60th birthday when she plans to retire. That's another 39 years of investing.

Now 39 years of investing should mean serious business. You'd expect that Wilma's £100 a month for 39 years should soon overtake the £25 a month that Fred's folk stashed away for just 21 years. After all, it's four times the money, being saved regularly for nearly twice as long. Stands to reason.

So, starting at the age of 21, let's see how it all pans out over the next few decades for Fred and Wilma's personal investments. And to make the comparison fair, we'll assume that Wilma achieves the same 9.8 per cent on her regular investments, and that Fred still earns the 9.8 per cent for the next 39 years on the lump sum that his parents accumulated for him. . .

AGE	FRED	WILMA
	£0	£100
	9.8%	9.8%
21	£19,724	£0
30	£62,057	£17,004
40	£158,058	£63,243
50	£402,569	£181,012
60	£1,025,331	£480,966

Just look at that! While we might have expected Wilma (who is saving four times as much per month as Fred ever did, remember) to catch up with and rapidly overtake Fred (who is adding zilch to his pile), she never gets close, does she?

In fact, she is falling behind all the time. When they were both 21, Wilma was nearly £20,000 behind Fred. By the age of 30, Fred's lump sum has way outperformed Wilma's regular investments and she's now £45,000 behind. By 40, she has fallen further behind and is trailing Fred by £95,000. By fifty it's worse, and she lags by £220,000. And look at those age 60 figures!

By the age of 60, Wilma's fortune has fallen behind Fred's to the tune of over half a million pounds. Fred, despite being a wastrel for 39 years, has accumulated more than twice as much money as Wilma.

We could imagine that both our worthy subjects will live for hundreds of years and see just how far behind Wilma might get. But no matter how long they live, she'll never catch up with him. If we wait long enough, all the stars in the Universe will go out, and we'll finally find out whether or not the whole thing is going to stop expanding and collapse again into a Big Crunch. But Wilma will never accumulate as much money as Fred.

So there's no point in carrying on with the calculations then, is there? What's that? You want us to do one more calculation, over an absurdly long period, just to prove the point? Oh, OK then. Here's what the situation will look like when Fred and Wilma are 1,000 years old. . .

AGE	FRED	WILMA
1,000	£$(150*10^{42})$	£$(72*10^{42})$

Look a bit strange? All it means is that Fred will have '150 times 10 to the power of 42' pounds and Wilma will have '72 times 10 to the power of 42' pounds. Approximately, that is, anyway. And if you want to write it out in full, for Fred's stash you'll need to write down £150 followed by 42 zeros; and for Wilma's, £72 followed by 42 zeros.

Amazingly, Fred's 21 years of investing £25 per month is worth more than Wilma's subsequent 979 years of investing £100 per month, and Fred still has twice as much money as Wilma (not that there'd be enough atoms to make all the banknotes, mind).

Let's finish this chapter with the next Fool's Rule for Kids.

Rule 3)   Early years are more important than later years.

A lot more.

Oh, and we're not going to apologize for using the words 'a lot' a lot. When it comes to long-term investing, getting the little things right matters. A lot.

Warren Buffett, who's he?

We've heard that we need to be thinking about investing for the long term, for decades. And to make the most of the time available, we have seen that we need to start investing for our children as early as possible. Now, it's all very well trotting out all those numbers showing how many gazillions of pounds we can accumulate for them, but most of us would still harbour a lingering suspicion, wouldn't we? 'Yes, but millions of pounds? What, me?! Nah,' would be an understandable response. Because it's never the little people who get their hands on the money, is it?

But what would we say if we could find an example, if we could find a very wealthy individual who has made his fortune by investing early and staying in for the long term, someone who only ever invests in great companies and never gives way to the greed and fear that usually accompany short-term trading?

Warren Buffett is the man, and if you haven't heard of him before, you have now.

Warren Buffett is chairman of Berkshire Hathaway, an American investment company. A big one, in fact, and a very successful one at that. But Berkshire Hathaway isn't the kind of investment company that takes regular cash payments from customers and invests the money in the stock market, in the way that most investment companies do.

No, Berkshire Hathaway is really a holding company, and what it holds are large chunks of other companies; sometimes entire companies. Warren Buffett analyzes and buys whole companies (or significant parts of them) the same way he would go about buying just a small number of shares. In fact, one of Buffett's favourite bits of advice is that you should never buy shares in a company if you would not be happy to buy the entire company. His favoured holding period is frequently quoted as 'forever.'

Buffett's letter to shareholders

Warren Buffett's annual letter to the shareholders of Berkshire Hathaway is a legendary piece of investing folklore. Published with the company's Annual Report every year, the letter is posted on the company's Web site (at www.berkshirehathaway.com) for all to see, and we strongly recommend Foolish followers to take a little time every now and again to go and read one of them. They really do make great reading, and are not what you might expect from a company chairman at all. In fact, Buffett's letters alone will take you a good way towards the Motley Fool's three aims – to educate, amuse, and enrich.

Here's what Fool writer Maynard Paton, who is an avid follower of Buffett's investment style, has to say about the Sage's annual letters. . .

'Whereas a typical chairman's annual statement is more akin to a public relations exercise, where even the most mediocre of accomplishments can be awarded a very complimentary inter-pretation, Buffett is renowned for his honest, straightforward and amusing remarks on the performance of Berkshire Hathaway. Not only does he present Berkshire shareholders the annual story in the no-nonsense manner that he would expect to receive were he a "passive" co-owner of the business, but he also throws in the odd bit of investment guidance and opinion as well. Obviously, with Buffett worth countless billions, the value of which was accumu-lated solely through stock market investment, it pays to take notice of what he writes.'

The last time we checked the Web site, Buffett's letters going all the way back to 1977 were up there for your pleasure. Enjoy.

Buffet has done pretty well for himself, but how did he get there?

Starting Young: Warren Buffett was born in 1930, so he's getting on a bit now, but he has had 70 years of investing possibilities. Buffett was no academic genius at school (but then again, many masters of their fields, like Albert Einstein, have been similar in that respect), but he soon put his smart investment mind to work in the pursuit of financial success.

After school, the young Buffett did the usual newspaper round that schoolkids have done since time immemorial (well, since newspapers were invented, anyway). But he went a bit further than that. He also had a bit of success touting his own horse-racing tip sheet. And if you think that horse racing is no activity for a sensible long-term investor, then you'd be right, but remember that Buffett was just selling the tips and letting others do the gambling, effectively taking a rake-off from their betting stakes.

He also bought and sold pinball machines and all sorts of other things, and by the age of about fifteen was taking home around $40 a week. $40 was a fair bit of money in 1945. When he left high school a year later, Buffett had amassed around $5,000 and a chunk of land into the bargain. Now that's a pretty impressive start, don't you think?

Some time after obtaining a university degree in Finance, Buffett happened upon a rather remarkable book. The tome in question was *The Intelligent Investor*, and it was by Benjamin Graham. Buffett was hooked (and we have to say, the name *Benjamin Graham* evokes a warm feeling in the heart of many a rational long-term investor, as he is one of the most influential writers on investment ever).

Graham's approach was all about understanding the companies that you might want to invest in, and learning to work out a rational valuation of each one. Now, reasoned Graham, if you come upon a time when the shares in a company are selling for a significantly lower price than the valuation that you have calculated (assuming that your valuation is close to the long-term truth, that is), then if you buy some you are unlikely to go wrong. Eventually (and you might have to wait a good while), the true valuation of a company will come out and will be reflected in the share price.

Buffett rushed off to study with Graham at Columbia University, where he spent the next couple of years. When Graham retired, Buffett headed back home to Omaha, Nebraska and started up his own investment partnership at the geriatric age of 25. The rest, as they say, is history.

Investing Long Term: Over the next 13 years, Buffett's investment partnership managed to achieve average annual returns of 30 per cent, which is rather good, to put it mildly. To put that into perspective, £1,000 invested at the start of those 13 years, at that annual rate of return, would have grown into £30,000. That's a 30-fold increase in just 13 years.

Anyway, Buffett thought the market was peaking and didn't think that he could find much in the way of under-valued investments, so he disbanded the partnership. He sold off all his holdings except two, one of which was Berkshire Hathaway, at that time a textile manufacturer. Some of Buffett's partners took the money and sold out at $43 per share, the going rate at the time. Others kept their money with Berkshire Hathaway, now under the control of Buffett.

Today (April 2000) those shares are worth around $60,000 apiece, and the whole company is worth more than $90 billion. That is what investing in good companies and holding your shares for a long time can do for your wealth.

But what of Buffett himself and what of Berkshire Hathaway's holdings?

Let's look at a few of Berkshire Hathaway's long-standing stock market investments, illustrated in the following table. . .

COMPANY	COST	MARKET VALUE 31/12/99
	($M)	($M)
American Express	1,470	8,402
Coca-Cola	1,299	11,650
Gillette	600	3,954
Washington Post	11	960
Wells Fargo	349	2,391

As we can see from the initial costs of the investments, when Buffett buys into a company, he buys big. But look at the results. It is also enlightening to see how long those investments have been held for.

Buffett started buying shares in Coca Cola in 1988 and has bought more over the years. Today, 12 years on from the first investment in the company, his total investment is worth nearly nine times the total purchase price.

$600 million worth of shares in Gillette were bought in 1991 and they're still there today, worth six and a half times as much.

Wells Fargo was bought in 1990, and has increased in value nearly sevenfold.

American Express is a pretty recent investment, the first chunk of it having been bought as recently as 1994, but the value of Berkshire's total holding has still risen nearly sixfold.

But perhaps the most impressive of the lot is The Washington Post Company. That investment was made in 1974 and 25 years later, by December 1999, had seen an 87-fold increase in its valuation.

However, 1999, a year in which Western stock markets were dominated by the rise of Internet and other technology companies, was actually a relatively poor year for Berkshire Hathaway. Buffett, you see, doesn't understand technology companies and so has never invested in any.

Anyway, coming back to compound returns, just think

what Buffett would have achieved if he had encountered Ben Graham when he was ten years old. We can't promise that you'll invest as well as Buffett on behalf of your child, but you can at least give them the benefit of all that extra time.

The chessboard answer

OK, back to the chessboard question. If you are the astute type, you probably wouldn't have needed to do any hard work at all to get to the right answer; all you needed was a little lateral thinking. You would, of course, have gone for the pennies on the chessboard. And how would you have arrived at your decision? Well, if that wasn't the right answer, we wouldn't have bothered asking the question really, would we?

But what is each of the three options actually worth?

The first option, £250 million, is easy. It's worth, erm, £250 million.

Option two is a better one though – 60 years' worth of compound interest at 20 per cent per year on £100 a month is worth a little over £338 million.

When we get to option three, though, we're really motoring. That penny on the first square, two pence on the second square, doubled up all the way to the 64th square is worth. . . are you ready for this? It's worth a rather impressive. . .

£184,467,440,737,095,000

That's around ten thousand times the total world economic output, so your mysterious benefactor would have to be an alien with a couple of galaxies at its disposal. That, or a liar.

Chapter Four: Why shares are best

After adjusting for inflation, we calculate that a £100 investment in an equity fund in 1869 would now be enough to buy a substantial house. The gilt or cash fund, however, might not even pay one year's council tax on the property.
Credit Suisse First Boston Equity-Gilt Study, 2000

At the Motley Fool, we have been using the Barclays Capital Equity-Gilt Study (www.barcap.com/egs/) for quite some time now as a source of information on stock market returns this century. In fact, this rather excellent report forms the cornerstone of our commitment to the stock market as the best form of long-term investment in existence; the best by a long way.

What those fine people at Barclays Capital did was study the returns of three main types of investment: equities (which just means share-based investments), gilts (a kind of government bond that is considered to be as safe as, er, a very safe thing), and cash in a savings account. They did this for every single year from 1918 until the present day, and calculated all sorts of interesting (nay, amazing) statistics like, for example, the returns from all three types of investments for every rolling five-year period covered by the study (which means 1918–23, 1919–24, 1920–25, and so on).

The results were staggering. Basically, what they found was that over the long term, equity investments wiped the floor with all other forms of investment. In fact, they wiped the floor, swept up the dust, and gave it the once-over with Mr Sheen.

This year, there's a new Barclays Capital Equity-Gilt Study out which extends the study to cover the whole of the 20th century, from December 1899 to December 1999.

And that's not all. The people over at Credit Suisse First Boston have published their own Equity-Gilt Study too (found at **www.csfb.com/eqres/eqres_gilt.html**), which traces the returns on shares, gilts and cash all the way back to 1869!

Both studies are well worth reading, and are pretty much guaranteed to open your eyes. This chapter's opening quote is taken from the CSFB study, and it should give you a feel for the findings. Impressed? Well, here are just a few of the results it uncovers. . .

Lump-sum investments

In the 25 years ending 31 December 1999, the average value of shares increased 149-fold. In comparison, gilts increased only 29-fold and cash sitting in a savings account came nowhere near. Now, to be fair, the strength of that particular comparison might be a little misleading, and that is because it starts at the beginning of 1974. Those of us old enough to remember might recall that 1974 wasn't one of the best year's on record for the stock market. In fact, it was one of the worst – it marked the bottom of a stock market 'crash'.

So, instead, let's move the goalposts back five years and look at the 25-year period from 1969 to 1994. That way we will cover all the years of the slump. And we will also remove the last five years, from 1994 to 1999, over which we saw a very strong stock market performance.

OK then, in the 25 years from 1969 to 1994, shares increased in value 36-fold with gilts showing a relatively sedate 14-fold growth.

Now, people trying to show how well the stock market has performed relative to other forms of investment might be expected to choose the best periods to use for their comparisons. But we're not like that, we prefer to be honest and let the facts speak for themselves. So, instead of looking for the best periods of stock market growth, let's see if we can find the worst periods this century.

The 1929 crash would probably spring to most people's minds when trying to think of a bad spell for the stock market, so how about the 25-year period ending in December 1929? Over those 25 years, average share values rose sixfold. That's not much compared to what we see in the good years, but by comparison, an investment in gilts over the same period would have managed a return of just 50 per cent.

How about what is probably the one other really bad period for shares, the one ending in that fateful year of 1974 that we mentioned earlier? In the 25 years to December 1974, the average value of shares increased sevenfold while gilts managed a return of a mere 26 per cent.

And just for fun, how would a really long-term investment, one that spans the whole of the period under scrutiny, have fared? Suppose we invested £100 in the stock market in 1869 and achieved average stock market returns over that period. How much would we have had at the end of 1999?

Now, you really need to be sitting down before you read the answer. Ready? OK, that £100 invested in 1869 would now be worth a rather cool £20 million. But inflation surely counts for a lot of that increase, doesn't it? So to get a real feel for the kind of wealth we are talking about we need to compare inflation-adjusted like with like. That £20 million, then, is still worth £500,000 in 1869 terms, which gives us a 5,000-fold growth in the real value of an average investment in the stock market over the 130 years. Or to put it another way, that is the equivalent of investing £4,000 today and watching it grow to £20 million in today's terms.

We are not, of course, suggesting that you stash away some money in the stock market at the birth of each new baby, and then leave it in some sort of trust until they each reach their 130th birthday. No, that would be taking the long-term approach just a tiny bit too far, even for us. But doesn't it make you reflect on how a lot of today's wealthy families might have acquired their fortunes? Suppose you stash away a proportion of your money for your kids for a couple of decades and then hand it over to them, and suppose they in turn stash a portion of their money (a portion of the money they earn themselves plus a cut of the money you accumulated for them) for their own kids. And so on. If the last 130 years is anything to go by, it shouldn't take too many generations before your descendants start to get really rather wealthy.

Think of that stately home of the future, with your portrait taking pride of place over the hearth in the Great Hall. 'That's great-great-great-grandma and grandpa that is,' they'll say, patting their bulging wallets, 'the founders of the great family fortune.' What a way to be remembered!

Regular investments

The evidence sounds good so far, but it gets better. If you are saving regularly over a long period, adding a little bit more to the pot every month, say, then you aren't going to fall into the old 'invest the lot at the start of a bad spell and get a relatively poor return' problem that would have affected someone starting such a strategy back in mid-1929.

Investing regularly has the effect of smoothing out the peaks and troughs in the stock market, and making it even more likely that you'll perform close to the long-term average, no matter when you start and finish (just providing you do it for long enough). Known as *pound cost averaging* (see the section about this further on), it is a simple effect that means you end up buying more investment units (shares, in this case) when the price is lower and fewer when the price is higher.

And the CSFB study kindly produces some figures that nicely show us the effects of regular savings over the last 30 years. But as well as providing incontrovertible evidence to show what our stock market returns would have been, the study also serves to show us the unimportance of getting the timing right, and what little difference it makes.

Let's say you invested £100 in shares on the first day of every year since 1969 and achieved average results. By the end of 1999, the value of that investment would have reached £88,315, which isn't at all bad for just £100 per year. By comparison, £100 invested each year in gilts over the same period would have netted you a final sum of £30,328, and cash would have given you £17,644. After adjusting for inflation, the equivalent figures come out at £21,236 for shares, £8,693 for gilts, and £5,376 for cash. That's a pretty ringing endorsement for shares, and a rather tidy return on a total investment of £3,000.

But what was all that stuff about timing not making much difference?

Let's go back to 1969, and start our £100 per year long-term investment again. However, this time, instead of investing it on the first day of each year, suppose you try to time the market. But you are phenomenally unlucky (you know, like the local soup factory announces a free soup day if you take your own utensils, but all you can find is a colander and a fork; that kind of unlucky), and you end up investing your £100 on the worst day of every year. Year in, year out, for 30 years, you manage to get in at the highest point of the market every single time. Now that, surely, will make a big difference, won't it?

Nope.

When the thirty years are up, your shares would be worth £74,302, which is £14,013 down on investing at the start of every year. That might sound like a big difference, but it is still far more than you would have got with gilts. Investing in gilts on the worst possible day every year, you would have accumulated only £22,921. A cash investment would have turned out the same, of course, at £17,644.

Thinking of this another way, if you invested in the stock market with such astoundingly bad luck in your timing, you would still end up with two and a half times as much money as you would have got investing in gilts on the first day of each year. The stock market 'worst-case' scenario still hammers the 'average' gilt example.

One last thought

Let's take a quick look at Barclays' new Equity-Gilt Study. They reckon that when looking at those rolling five- and ten-year periods (1899-1904, 1900-1905, etc), shares out-performed cash in 77 per cent of all five-year periods and in 92 per cent of all ten-year periods. And our own perusal of the CSFB report has failed to turn up a single 15-year period in which shares did not outperform both gilts and cash.

What all this means is that over time – one of the things your children hopefully have plenty of – shares are incontrovertibly the best investment.

Pound cost averaging

It might sound like a fiendishly clever investing strategy, but pound cost averaging is just what happens, inevitably and without you even realizing it, whenever you make regular investments over a period of time in which the market is fluctuating. And the market always fluctuates. To see how it works, we'll take a simplified example.

Suppose you are investing £100 a month in an index tracker, and the units are priced at £1 each. You'll be getting 100 units per month, then. Now suppose the index doesn't budge for six months and the unit price doesn't change from £1. After six months, you'll have bought 600 units. Simple enough. But now, there's some major world catastrophe somewhere, the stock market drops by 50 per cent, and the units in your index tracker fall in price to 50p. Nothing changes for the next six months and the price stays steady at 50p (see, we told you it was a simplified example). After the second six months you will have bought a further 1,200 units and will be sitting on a total of 1,800 units. Now what is your average price? The simple average price of the units over the year is 75p.

But you'll have done better than that – the average price you will have paid will only be 66.6p, because you bought twice as many at the lower price. Your average is calculated as £1,200 (your total investment) divided by 1,800 (the total number of units you have bought).

In this example, we look at a crash followed by a recovery, but it would have worked out exactly the same had the market fluctuated rapidly, with the price alternating each month between £1 and 50p. All you needed was six months in total at each price to get that average.

Now assume that our imagined crisis is over and the stock market rebounds to where it was at the start of the year. This might sound contrived, but it is what actually happens when the stock market falls; it bounces back to its former level and beyond before too long. Now the price of your units is back to £1, and you have 1,800 of them. If the stock market hadn't fallen, you would have only bought 1,200 units, so you are already 50 per cent up simply due to a short-term stock market fall.

So remember, in the long term, the stock market rises. And short-term dips are good for regular long-term investors because they add a bit extra on to our annual returns.

Chapter Five: Avoiding the dross

My daughter's stupid. She chose numbers 1,2,3,4,5 and 6.
What are the chances of that combination ever winning the
Lottery?
Overheard on a bus

Investing for children, from as early an age as possible, really does sound like rather a good thing to do, don't you think? What?! You've read all about the compounding of returns and you don't want your kids to get that much money because it might go to heir heads?

Oh, you're only joking. Good.

Seriously, as well as making you a very, very popular parent (or uncle or aunt, or guardian, or just a very generous friend), stashing away a big sack of loot for them will give you the satisfaction of knowing that when the kids that you care about reach adulthood, you'll have given them a solid leg-up in leading a creative and fulfilled life. Which is what we all want for our kids, no?

Now, having seen how an investment with a return of, say, 10 per cent per year will significantly outperform investments returning 8 per cent or 6 per cent or less per year, an obvious question must spring to mind. (Actually, it may have sprung to mind ages ago, and you've been patiently ploughing through the book thinking, 'Come on then, I'm convinced, spare me all these endless examples and numbers, and tell me how to go about doing do it!')

Yep, that's the question, 'How do I go about investing for the children in my life?'

OK, it's time to examine a number of different investment possibilities, and we will look at how well each one suits the long-term investor. A whole host of diverse and wonderful devices have been thought up over the decades for enriching children, and each generation seems to have had its own favourites. It has been pretty rare, though, for one generation's favourite investment to remain the favourite with the next generation. But why is that? Perhaps it's because, where their parents have invested for them at all, each generation has been the unwitting victim of their parents' well-meaning but often misguided investment attempts.

Each generation's favourite savings scheme has been pretty much dictated by the prevailing Wise investment fashion of the day, and parents have used these popular investment methods simply because they haven't known any better. It has been in the interests of Wise investment advisers since time immemorial to keep things that way. Until recently, very little real information about long-term investment was available to the general public, and even if the relevant information could be accessed, the world of stock market investment was pretty much a closed shop. Only the well-heeled, brolly-carrying, pin-stripe brigade had access to stockbrokers, and dealing in shares cost a pretty penny too.

In fact, it was only the stock market 'Big Bang' of 1986 that really started the ball rolling. Fortunately, we see a far more deregulated stock market today, with many more companies able to offer us their brokerage services via whichever medium we choose, and to charge whatever the competitive market demands. Before deregulation, brokers were actually obliged to stick to a set scale of fees, and they weren't low. Cheap and easy access to stockbrokers has only really become available to ordinary private investors in the last decade or so.

But many people still stick to the old ways, regardless of the actual merits of their chosen investments, and wouldn't give the stock market a second's thought.

This chapter, then, is dedicated to looking at some favourite places to stash the kids' cash, old and new.

The Lottery

The advent of the National Lottery brought about something of a cultural change in Britain. Once those funny little balls had first bounced around in that machine that looks like a prop from a cheap science fiction film, and the first seven had popped out, Saturday evenings were changed for ever for countless people up and down the country. And now we have the cursed thing on Wednesdays too.

Many of us must be tempted to put a couple of quid on each time for the kids. But what does that represent as an investment? Not very much really. With the odds of winning the big one coming in at around 14 million to one against, the chances of striking it rich for your young ones are slim in the extreme.

One problem with the Lottery is that it is a less than zero sum game, and a fair bit less comes out to the players than goes in. What that means is that, long term, you're guaranteed to lose. Yes, even those lucky few who have already struck it big will lose the lot if they keep playing long enough. OK, that's not much of a worry for them, as they'd have to keep playing for twenty or thirty thousand years or more to lose it all, but it's a thought to bear in mind.

Is the Lottery something for Fools to be interested in for their children? No, not as an investment. If you enjoy the excitement, then go and play it by all means, but don't waste you children's money that way.

Lottery lore

The author remembers the very first draw of the UK National Lottery quite clearly. As I was sitting on a bus on the Monday morning after the draw, there was a bunch of people sitting just a few seats in front discussing the new phenomenon.

One of them commented on how close she'd been to becoming Britain's very first Lottery millionaire. She only actually got a couple of numbers right, but every other number drawn had been oh so close to hers. Now, there must be thousands of people up and down the country who suffer the same ill fortune every Wednesday and Saturday, and curse the fates in similar vein. But just think about it for a moment, logically. If you choose, say, number 23 and ball number 24 pops out, was that close? There's no way to tell, because ball number 23 could have been anywhere, and instead of being close you might actually have been out a good nine inches or more.

Suppose that instead of numbers, the balls had girls' and boys' names on them. Do you reckon that there'd be busloads of people going to work on Mondays and Thursdays cursing their bad luck in quite the same way?

'You know, I was sooo close. I chose Malcolm and it came out Rosemary.'

Probably not. It's exactly the same though, because those numbers confer no more of a relationship between different balls than the use of people's names would.

But that wasn't all. Another of the bunch came out with the cracker that is now the opening quote at the start of this chapter. The temptation to answer, 'Why, approximately 14 million to one against, exactly the same as any other selection of six numbers,' was almost too strong to resist.

Premium bonds

Premium bonds used to be a big favourite a generation or so ago, and a bond or two from Grandma and Grandpa was often one of the presents that a newcomer to this world might expect to receive. What pleased the older folk back then was the fact that the money was protected and could never be lost, because they were rather fearful of risk in those days; the idea of losing any money, even short term, was cause for palpitations of the severest kind. And you never knew, there was always the chance of a top-up in the form of a win from good old ERNIE from time to time.

But wins are pretty rare, and inflation destroys the value of the so-called 'protected' capital; and together that makes for a poor average rate of return. With a regular trickle of small prizes, Premium Bond fans who never win the big one can expect to achieve a long-term average return of around 3 per cent per year. That is tax free, of course, so it would be the equivalent of a 5 per cent gross return for a higher-rate taxpayer (which still wouldn't be anything to shout about). But if your children are already higher-rate taxpayers, then perhaps you should think about getting them to invest for you instead. In fact, as we shall see later, the 'tax-free' label will usually count for nothing at all for most children's investments.

And who is to blame for so many well-meant gifts to children ending up in such a poorly-performing investment? Those Wise advisers in the financial services industry, that's who, as it is they who, for so long, have done such a good job of scaring people away from better long-term investments.

So Premium Bonds aren't for Foolish children either.

Kevin's uncle

Kevin, a friend of the author, had an uncle. Well, he had more than one uncle actually, but there's only one that we're really interested in here. Kevin's uncle, you see, was a devotee of Premium Bonds. That in itself is not unusual, as people of Kevin's uncle's generation were brought up on Premium Bonds. Knowing that your money was safe and you'd be guaranteed to always get it back no matter how long you left it there had an understandable appeal to a very safe and thrifty generation, and a generation with little in the way of useful education about the nature of probabilities at that . . .

So in this, Kevin's uncle was by no means unique. No, it was his Premium Bond selection method that might make a Fool smile a little today. You see, Kevin's uncle always bought his Premium Bonds in blocks of consecutive numbers; never as lone individuals scattered throughout the number range. Fair enough, one might suppose, but Kevin's uncle did it this way because he believed that it actually improved his chances of winning! What? Yes, and his reasoning went along the lines of. . .

How often do you hear of people winning big prizes? Not very often. But how often do you hear of people being close, just a few numbers out? A lot more often than you hear of people actually winning. Well then, he reasoned, if you buy a large block of numbers instead of scattered individual ones, you stand a much better chance of turning those near misses into big wins.

Try as he might to explain probability theory and how every Premium Bond has an exactly equal chance of being chosen regardless of its actual bond number, Kevin couldn't dent his uncle's faith in his system even a tiny bit.

Still, if he wasn't really improving his chances at all, at least he wasn't doing them any harm. And if Kevin's uncle was happy doing it that way, then good for him.

Mind you, he never won a penny.

National Savings

After the Premium Bond generation, National Savings accounts scored a big hit with the next wave of parents, and it's not that hard to see why they became so popular. At the time, today's widespread use of bank accounts was still a long way off, and many people's income still came in the form of a weekly wage packet stuffed with actual cash. Bank accounts were for the wealthy, and local branches were staffed with assistants and bank managers whose pomposity could rival that of Mr Mainwaring.

Post Offices, though, were friendly local places. And the idea of putting away the odd shilling or two into the children's Post Office books every now and then was an attractive proposition.

Putting something away for a rainy day was considered very important in those far-off debt-averse days (and it's such a shame that this particular philosophy is now losing popularity, and that personal borrowings are increasing so much); and the fact that interest on National Savings was paid free of tax added to the incentive. The idea, though, that ordinary folk could actually generate a reasonable pile over the years was pretty much an alien one to most.

How have investments in National Savings fared over the years? The current rate of interest is approximately 1.8 per cent per year on an ordinary National Savings account, with the long-term average over the last couple of decades coming in at around 2 per cent. There are higher rates of interest available from other types of accounts, but most require some sort of minimum investment period. An Investment Account, for example, currently pays out 4.5 per cent per year on balances up to £500, and 4.6 per cent on balances up to £2,500, but you do need to give one month's notice to get money out without losing some interest. That's better, but as a long-term investment, it really doesn't cut it.

You can also invest in National Savings Children's Bonus Bonds, if you really want to. These are fixed-term five-year investments, and they offer a fixed return guaranteed for the five years. There's a bonus at the end of the five years, too. The rate of interest on these bonds currently comes in at 5.65 per cent per year (after including the terminal bonus), which, again, is a pretty poor return for a long-term investment. And the maximum you can invest is £1,000 anyway, which might sound like a lot if you are just starting out with a new baby, but we've already seen just how much a modest regular investment can turn into given a decent rate of return. If you invest Foolishly for your children, that £1,000 limit could soon start to look like chicken feed.

The tax-free status of children's bonds is often touted as a great reason for buying them, but your children are very unlikely to be paying much tax on their investment earnings anyway, so that's a red herring to ignore.

Yorick's tale

Another friend of the author's, Yorick, recently had cause to ponder the stunning lack of riches that National Savings accounts have generated over the long term.

When moving house a little while ago, in 1999, he found a long-lost Post Office book; an account that had been opened for him 22 years previously. The last entry in the book, dated 1977, showed an outstanding balance of a little over £3.50. Curious to know how this little nest egg had performed over the subsequent 22 years, he rushed off to get the book updated. And the results? The 22 years of interest amounted to the seriously underwhelming sum of £2.50, representing a compounded annual rate of approximately 2 per cent.

'And to think, I could have seen Star Wars twice at the cinema on that £3.50 back in 1977,' was the only comment to be heard from him.

Oh, and Yorick also says that he still has £2 in Premium Bonds that his grandparents bought for him when he was born. And he hasn't won a penny more than Kevin's uncle.

Endowments and other insurance wonders

Endowments, now there's a thing. Many of us can remember a time when parents would tuck a couple of quid a week into a policy that the doorstep salesman promised would provide an attractive lump sum at a specific age, 18 or 21 or whatever. That lump sum could be used to help provide further education, or to go on a holiday to celebrate the offspring flying the nest, or anything you wanted. It sounded so attractive at the time, when that nice official-looking man in a smart suit told us how important it was to save for our children's futures. In that much, he was right, but that's all he was right about.

Were those policies a good deal? How many of us can remember our parents getting those lump sums back, and how much did they get? If you had a new bouncing baby back in, say, 1960, an 18-year policy that promised to pay back £100 or £150 18 years later might have sounded like a good deal, and you'd get insurance thrown in too. But 18 years later, your kid has grown up and that £150 isn't enough to help contribute to the costs of further education, or cover the budding Kray's bail bond, or whatever. And that's because the actual annual return on your monthly payments has barely managed to match inflation, with all those monthly payments gaining little in the way of compound returns.

Imagine if that nice young salesman had been a bit more honest and open in his sales pitch. It might have gone something like this. . .

Salesman:	Hello, I'm Mr Chargetoomuch.
Fool:	Pardon?
Salesman:	Mr Chargetoomuch; I'm here to sell you an endowment.
Fool:	How does that work, then?
Salesman:	Firstly, we work out how much you can afford to invest every month.
Fool:	Yes.
Salesman:	And you give that to us.
Fool:	And what happens then?
Salesman:	Well, for the first two years, we'll keep it.
Fool:	What? Why?
Salesman:	We've got to look after your investment for 18 years, so we need to be paid.

Fool:	What, 18 years' pay up front? All of it?
Salesman:	Yes, that's right.
Fool:	And you don't actually invest any money for me until you've taken all your charges?
Salesman:	Correct again.
Fool:	But what if I want to stop part-way through; will you refund a portion of your charges?
Salesman:	No, we'll keep the 18 years' charges, even if we've only done a few years' work.
Fool:	And the rest?
Salesman:	Well, the chances are you'll get back less that you've actually paid in, if you stop early.
Fool:	And if I keep going, will I get that terminal bonus that you promised?
Salesman:	Only if you're very lucky. And I never promised anything.

If that was the way they really sold endowments, such a conversation wouldn't have gone on much further, would it? Imagine if you went to your boss one Monday morning and announced that, because you expect to be working for the company for another 30 years, you want your next 30 years' pay up front. And if your boss decides to sack you (because, let's face it, after you've got your 30 years' pay up front, there's not much incentive to work hard, is there?), then you obviously won't be refunding any of that advance pay. Think your boss would fall for it? No, of course not. But that endowment salesman was pulling exactly the same trick.

So, what do you reckon? Do you think an endowment would make a good investment?

If you think not, you are not alone.

Think of all of those people who have been sold an endowment-based mortgage. The situation is exactly the same: you invest your money in a 'with-profits' insurance vehicle in the hope that it will provide a big enough lump sum at some future date to cover a specific expense (in this case, the capital you borrowed to buy your house). According to recent estimates, however, between half a million and three million people who have endowment-based mortgages are unlikely to get enough out of them to pay for their houses. Knowing this probably doesn't make you want to trust your children's investment money to an insurance company.

If we think about it, why on earth should we want to combine the purchase of insurance with making an investment in the first place? When we are buying a car, do we look for a deal that includes buying our annual holidays? Or do we combine our grocery shopping with dental treatment? No. So why combine insurance with investment?

Still not convinced? Here's what a Fool, known as Samaya, said in a message on the *Investing For Kids* discussion board a little while back. . .

> *Having a wild and wacky idea when I was three months' pregnant, I decided to invest for the blobling. You will have to forgive me, but I spoke to a 'Wise' one and I was advised to invest in the Clerical Medical with-profits regular payment fund. I have been paying into this, a fair amount, since March 1996. In January 1999 I requested a current plan value, as they had failed to furnish me with any correspondence since the onset of this! To my horror/ amazement/annoyance the value of the fund was less than half of what had been paid in. Not impressed. . . I do believe strongly I was given a bum steer.*

Our Foolish friend wasn't too impressed by her endowment (for that is what it was) and neither should you be if that's the kind of return they provide.

So, if you want to buy insurance (and it is a good thing to have in appropriate amounts and for appropriate things), buy it for what it is – a safeguard against misfortune. If you want a decent investment, though, put your money somewhere else.

Friendly Societies

Friendly Societies have been in existence in the UK for over 150 years, and originated when local groups of people got together to form mutual savings societies, pooling resources to take care of future rainy days. Such societies are quite often touted as a good place to invest money for your children, but do they give you a good deal?

Friendly Societies do enjoy some tax breaks. In fact, everyone is entitled to hold one Friendly Society savings plan, the proceeds of which are not taxable; but they have certain limitations. Friendly Society savings plans generally last ten years (with the exception of children's, which can be kept in place until they are 18 or 21), and the maximum you can invest is set at £25 per month. The gains from any growth and maturity bonuses are exempt from tax.

Too good to be true? Well, no, not really. There are two big problems. Friendly Societies' charges tend to be rather high – a cut of £2 per month out of that £25 maximum is not uncommon (and that's up to 8 per cent lost in charges before you get any growth at all).

Secondly, these plans are often based on insurance products. Yes, that's right, many of them are just another form of endowment. And, as we have seen, endowments don't have an exactly sparkling record when it comes to earning good rates of return. So, with the typically high charges, and the typically low performance, you'll be lucky if your investment keeps pace with inflation. A tax-exempt return isn't really much use if that return is a poor one in the first place, is it?

Some Friendly Societies do offer 'unit-based' savings plans, which are actually stock market-based investments. But you will almost certainly find that the money is invested in a very conservative, high-charging, poorly performing fund. You shouldn't usually expect a Friendly Society to get you even close to the average stock market return, once all the charges, commissions and poor performance have been taken into account.

And if that wasn't enough, the tax saving means nothing for children anyway. This is because the same amount of money invested every month in, say, a stock market index tracker fund (of which more later) under the protection of a bare trust (and again, we'll meet these beasts later), is unlikely to be taxable anyway, as children have their own income and capital gains tax allowances to use up.

But how about an example? Here's what a regular Fool discussion board contributor, who goes by the name of Hoolio, had to say of such an experience. . .

> *Most unwelcome leaflet. It was from the 'Family Assurance Society' (I forget the exact name) and touted a financial product called the 'Junior Bond'. Once you'd ploughed through the pictures of happy toddlers, 'give them the best start in life', free gifts when you join, etc., you find out in the small print that £10 a month for 10 years (total £1200) at growth of 6 per cent (estimated) would yield you . . . wait for it . . . a truly scandalous £1265. In other words, nothing at all. . . well to be fair, they take 5 per cent of the growth in fees and you get the 1 per cent remainder. How can such a product be allowed to be sold to new mums and dads like this?*

So Fools should steer clear of these investments, because saving the tax on such appallingly bad returns is an economy of the falsest nature.

Private Education Bonds

You'll see companies offering things they call Private Education Bonds, too. The idea of these is that you make regular monthly savings for your children, and that the money is invested over the years to pay for private education later in life. But they are usually just another form of endowment or insurance vehicle in disguise. There are no tax breaks, no specific allowances, no nothing at all in fact.

So what you are getting is an ordinary, common or garden, low-performance policy. The 'education' bit is a complete red herring (and you could be forgiven for thinking that this a book about fantasy fish, the number of these we have come across so far), and it makes absolutely no difference whatsoever to your contributions or to your returns. It's just a bit of window dressing; something to make it all sound good and distract you from the usually appalling returns on offer.

Friendly Societies are among the institutions that try to peddle this particular brand of snake oil, but we've already seen how poor their performance usually is.

Forward ho

So, we've managed to debunk a few popular favourites.

'But come on, surely there is something that the Fool approves of, isn't there?' you might ask. Well, there is, and we'll move on to savings accounts next. Your child will probably need one of those, even if it's only for short-term accumulation of cash before the funds get transferred to proper long-term investments.

Chapter Six: Banks And Building Societies

It is better that a man should tyrannize over his bank balance than over his fellow citizens.
John Maynard Keynes

Banks. Love 'em or hate 'em, we can't ignore them. As part of a rational long-term investing strategy, a savings account of some sort is going to be a very important part of handling your children's cash. If you are going to invest for the long term, you'll need somewhere to save those small amounts of money while they build up into a large enough chunk to invest properly. And even if you're making a regular monthly investment on their behalf directly into, say, a stock market index tracker fund, they'll still get birthday and Christmas cash from Aunt Petunia and Uncle Groucho, and you don't want that to be frittered away on Pokémon monsters and Playstation games, do you? Well, not all of it anyway.

So savings accounts are much-needed short-term cash depositories, but how do they shape up in the Motley Fool multi-decade investment stakes? This chapter mainly examines bank and building society accounts with a view to whether they represent good long-term homes for your children's money. The short-term picture – i.e. as simply a place to hold cash on an interim basis – is somewhat different, and we talk about this at the end of the chapter.

The Big Four

It can be quite an interesting exercise to pop into the local branches of the big four high street banks and ask a question along the lines of. . .

What's the best way to put away some regular savings for my six-year-old nephew, with the intention of continuing them until he's 18 years old?

And that is exactly what we did. We chose a Fool researcher at random (well, it was a random choice out of the one who was available, anyway), and placed this quest upon his stout Foolish shoulders.

'Go out into the unknown,' we urged him. 'Go into the dark halls of the Wise and sit at their tables. Consume their morsels and ask questions of their Wisdom. Commit their lore to memory and hasten back, laden with tales of their mythology and their machinations, so wondrous to tell.'

So off he went to the bank.

And with 'local' bank branches being a lot further away these days than they used to be, thanks to the increasing popularity of closing the things down, it used up a bit more shoe leather than was initially expected.

The chances were that our researcher would get a pretty similar answer from every one of the banks, and we expected something along the lines of, 'Why, a special *BarcWest* "Little Scrooge" kiddies savings account is what you need, and look at all the lovely goodies you get as a bonus when you open one.'

And our expectations were pretty much met, though the comparison of how much information each of the banks was willing to offer unprompted is interesting, and might be a reasonable indicator of how genuinely interested each one is in helping to get your kids switched on to the idea of saving money. Or it could just be a measure of how grumpy, depressed or out of sorts the unfortunate staff member you chose as your victim just happened to be that day. Whatever.

Anyway, our extensive Fool research survey (OK, a quick half hour poking around the nearest bank-laden high street, asking a few questions and grabbing a bagful of leaflets) took a look at each bank's offering in turn and attempted to evaluate them on both the quality of the product and the apparent quality of the service offered at the time.

So, in alphabetical order (not for any good reason, mind, but because it's as good an order as any), take it away you bankers. . .

Barclays: Finding anyone to talk to was a bit tricky, as the staff-to-customer ratio was a little on the low side at the chosen branch. The information desk was fully occupied with customers, engaged in obviously deep conversation on some matter of Wise importance, judging by the number of lines on their foreheads. Hmm, haven't really got time for this, so let's leave them to their brow-furrowing and see what's to be had from the counter. A couple of leaflets, that's what.

Ah well, it's a start, so let's examine those and see what they have to say. We can always go and have a look at their Web site for more details later. They must have a Web site, right?

Right then, what Barclays offer is two different versions of their children's account, one is called *BarclayPlus*, the other *Junior BarclayPlus*. The former is for children between the ages of 11 and 16, while the latter is for children under 11. Hmm, one immediate question springs to mind. Why two? And what's the difference? (OK, two questions then). Closer scrutiny is clearly called for, so let's see how the two accounts are described. . .

Junior:	'Who wants a funny animal with a hole in its back when you could have a real bank account?'
Big kids:	'We have spent time asking people your age what they expect from a bank.'"
Junior:	'However you eventually decide to spend your savings, with *Junior BarclayPlus* you can easily take out as much or as little as you want.'
Big kids:	'With *BarclayPlus* you can manage your money yourself, deciding exactly how you want to spend it.'

Junior:	'We'll make sure that as long as you have £10 or more in your account, it will earn interest.'
Big kids:	'As long as you have £10 or more in your account we will pay you interest.'
Junior:	'Interest is added four times a year.'
Big kids:	'. . .which we will credit to your account every three months.'

Wow! That's clear then. The differences between the two accounts are as clear as, well, something that isn't actually very clear at all. But come on, there must be a difference. There must be some reason for going to all the trouble of printing up two whole batches of different leaflets.

Ah, here it is. . . Big kids 'can apply for a *BarclayPlus* card (with parental approval), so you can get money from our cash machines.'

Is that it? Is that the only difference? Are they really trying to make out that they have two separate accounts, one for older kids and one for younger kids, each specifically tailored to its target age group, when all they mean is, 'And when you reach age 11, you can have a *BarclayPlus* card too'? Well, it certainly looks that way.

And what about, 'We have spent time asking people your age what they expect from a bank'? Do they really think that today's teenagers can be patronized so badly and still come running to their door crying, 'Thank you Barclays, nobody ever listened to us until you came along'?

What people need from a savings account has got nothing to do with their age. Two things are needed from a savings account – a decent interest rate and easy access to the money. That's it, there's nothing else. So come on Barclays, give us a break.

We had to smile a little though, when we read more about the *BarclayPlus* card. Apparently, if you're under 16, it can only be obtained with parental approval. But you can't have a *BarclayPlus* account at all once you're over 16! Oh dear, the leaflet only has four pages of actual content, so we might have thought a little consistency wouldn't be beyond them.

We wondered about tax too (kids shouldn't pay it, you see). But the only thing the leaflet said was, 'Contact Barclays for details.' Grrrr.

And what about the interest rate? They didn't offer any details in their leaflets. And that Web site? Well, our Foolish researcher couldn't find anything about current interest rates at all, so just sat there ridiculing the site's 'serious fun for young people' approach, with its graphic-intensive pages (which means slow) that each contain a tiny amount of information. The 'information per click' count is one of the lowest he's seen, apparently. And who needs a kids' jokes page from a bank, after all?

So a phone call was needed to find out the rate of interest, which turns out to be a staggeringly unimpressive 2.0 per cent gross return p.a., and that's only for balances of £100 or over; with £99 or less in the account, you only get 1.5 per cent. Hardly what we want when it comes to building long-term wealth, is it?

Verdict time. . .

Barclays said: 'Who wants a funny little animal with a hole in its back when you could have a real bank account?'

Our survey said: 'Bye bye, Barclays.'

HSBC: This one started off a bit better, and there were a couple of staff available to help with questions. So our researcher consulted the oracles (the ones sitting at the information desk) and probed deeply on all manner of mysteries. It went something like this. . .

Fool:	What's the best way to put away some regular savings for my six-year-old nephew, with the intention of continuing them until he's 18 years old?
HSBC:	This leaflet, *Young Savers Account*, will give you the details.

Fool: What about tax – how do you stop deducting it at source?

HSBC: You just need to fill in an Inland Revenue form. It tells you in the leaflet.

Fool: Do you offer any incentives for young savers?

HSBC: They get a free money box that looks like a little red safe. It tells you about it in the leaflet.

Fool: What about interest?

HSBC: You can have it paid quarterly or annually. We've included the latest rates in the leaflet.

Fool: Thanks, I'll have a think about it.

HSBC: Just one thing – it says in the leaflet that kids can have accounts in their own names at the age of seven. We actually do that for six-year-olds now.

Well the service seemed a bit better, and it even sounded like the leaflet might actually contain a bit of concrete information for a change. So back to Fool Regional HQ (Liverpool) to peruse the paperwork.

And we have to say, the HSBC leaflet wasn't patronizing, wasn't full of garish bright colours and pictures of carefully posed teenagers, and had none of this 'We have spent time asking people your age what they expect from a bank' nonsense. It didn't have much else either, mind, but it was reasonably refreshing to our Foolish researcher's jaded eyes.

But what about the details? Minimum £1 to get started, £10 to get the free money box. Anyone under 11 years old can have an account, with parents' or guardians' consent. And when you reach the age of seven (sorry, six, as the oracle pointed out), the account can be in your own name (with parental consent, of course).

And what if you're over 11? You know, the age when Barclays' *BarclayPlus* account cuts in? At HSBC, your account converts to a *Livecash* account, which gets you a cash card and frees you from having to get Mum or Dad to sign for you whenever you want to get some money out.

And tax? It says you need to fill in a copy of Inland Revenue form R85 (and it's right), which you can get from any branch.

Keeping the most important thing until last, then, what rate of interest do you get? Whether you have it paid annually or quarterly, you get a gross annual return of 4.25 per cent. That compares pretty favourably to HSBC's *Instant Access Savings* accounts, which only offer over 4 per cent for balances in excess of £25,000, but it doesn't score many points in the quest for long-term wealth enhancement.

So, a decent performance on the clarity and helpfulness front, but that interest rate loses it for long-term Fools.

What's the verdict?

HSBC said: 'You can get a free "safe" money box so you can have fun building pennies into pounds.'

Our survey said: 'Hardly, HSBC.'

Lloyds TSB: A popular bank with investors, and one that regularly posts better results than many of its competitors, but how does it handle queries about kids' accounts? There were a few people queuing at the windows, but the information desk was free. There was nobody there, and there was a bell marked 'Ring for Service'. So our researcher rang. And he stood there for a couple of minutes. Then another couple of minutes. No service was apparent. His eye was caught by a rack of leaflets not four feet away (well, actually, it was four feet away), and one stood out. '*Young Savers Account,* for the children in your life,' it proclaimed boldly. So he grabbed a copy and had a quick glance through it. Still nobody came to answer his desperate summons for service. So he rang again. Then he waited again for a couple of minutes. Then another couple of minutes – again. Then he had another look through the leaflet. Another minute passed, but there was still no service to be had. And the more he rang and waited, the more nobody came to help.

Oh well, they had their chance. But the banks all look to be pretty much the same anyway, and there's little more the staff can add to what's in the leaflets, so we'll just rely on that.

OK, the front cover says, 'Good rates of interest, no charges, and a free gift.' Hmm, the old free gift routine again, eh? Now where have we heard that one before? Let's turn the page. 'Important information for you,' it said, 'Lloyds Bank and TSB are joining forces on the 28th June 1999 to become Lloyds TSB.' Wow, we can hardly wait. But hang on a minute, it's April 2000 now, and that 'important information' is about as fresh as the turkey you're still eating six days after Christmas. This is not a promising start.

But what does the rest of the leaflet offer us? Here are a few tasters. . .

'You simply open the account in your own name on the child's behalf any time from their birth up to their tenth birthday – and manage it for them until they're sixteen.' Hmm, that seems a bit tough on parents who've got an eleven year old.

'When you open the account, we'll give you a present for the child: a colourful stationery set, complete with notepad, coloured pencils, set square, ruler, rubber and pencil sharpener.' Wow! That's us convinced. Who needs a decent rate of return when you can have a colourful stationery set? Seriously though, it hardly seems like an irresistible offer, not to us at least.

'To make the *Young Savers Account* worthwhile, every pound will earn an attractive rate of interest.' Well, we're glad it isn't only every other pound, or just pounds that you save on days when it's sunny.

'To find out our current rates, please call in at any branch.' What, and ring the bell at the information desk?

'Usually a child under sixteen can receive all their interest without any tax being deducted. When you open the account we'll give you an IR85 tax form,' it says. It's actually called an 'R85', but perhaps we shouldn't be too critical; typographical errors can happen to anyone. There are no doubt one or two in this book.

'And if you pay in foreign currency cheques worth up to

£100, we won't charge for converting the money to sterling.'
Now that's an interesting twist, and one that might be useful
to some parents, although it's worth noting that banks make
much of their money on currency transactions through the
difference in the buying and selling prices – which will no
doubt still apply here – and not from the commission. Still, a
Lloyds TSB *Young Savers Account* may make a useful clearing
house for foreign cheques. (Better wait and see if that still holds
once Lloyds Bank and TSB are joined, though. Ouch, OK,
sorry, we'll put our claws away now.)

And the all-important interest rate? A quick phone call after
returning to Fool HQ soon dug it up, and it was 5.0 per cent
at the time, which is a relatively decent rate of return. Relative
to the rest of the big four banks, that is. In fact, it is the highest
of the four, significantly ahead of NatWest and HSBC, and
streets ahead of Barclays.

The verdict this time?
Lloyds TSB said: 'The *Young Savers Account* gives a child a good
financial start in life.'
Our survey said: 'Long way to go, Lloyds.'

National Westminster: This is definitely a 'best until last'
story in terms of quality of service as far as the big four banks
go (though not in terms of interest rates). Our researcher's
oracular confabulations went something like this. . .

Fool:	What's the best way to put away some regular savings for my six-year-old nephew, with the intention of continuing them until he's 18 years old?
NatWest:	What we offer is our *Young Saver* account, which is available to all children up to the age of 11. As your nephew is under seven, the account will have to be in your name, but it can be transferred into his own name once he reaches the age of seven. Interest is currently around 4

per cent, which is pretty good. The exact figure is in this leaflet here, which also tells you all about the account. For children, interest can be paid gross of tax. All you need to do is fill in Inland Revenue form R85, and here's a copy for you. We also offer some start-up incentives providing you start with at least £10 in the account. The child will get a special folder to keep all his statements in, and it includes a wall chart and some stickers and things to help him keep a track of his money. And we also offer a voucher for a free Dorling Kindersley book, either an atlas for older children, or a book about numbers that's more suitable for younger ones. You'll have to send the voucher off yourself, but we've got copies of both books here if you want to see them.

Fool: Thanks, you've answered all my questions for now. I'll go and read the leaflet and maybe get back to you.

Well, NatWest has to score full marks for the helpfulness and friendliness of that particular member of staff, and the branch had a copy of the folder pack and the two books on hand to show customers. But what about the account itself? The leaflet is a bit glossy and colourful, but it avoids patronizing the kids and pretty much just states the facts.

Now, reasonably decent going from NatWest, and their free goodies are the best so far, but that all-important interest rate? It is, after all, the thing that really matters and NatWest comes in second of the big four pile, with an interest rate of 4.32 per cent gross.

But that 4.32 per cent compares unfavourably with Lloyds' figure of 5 per cent, and is nowhere near good enough for a fledgling Fool starting out on the long road to fortune.

So, the verdict. . .

NatWest said: 'With our *Young Saver* account you just sit back and watch their interest grow.

Our survey said: 'No cigar, NatWest.'

The Building Societies

Well, we're not too impressed with the high street banks really, so what about a few of the better-known building societies (and ex-building societies)? The difference between building societies and banks is becoming more and more blurred, of course, and the distinction will probably mean nothing in a few years' time. But for now the separation will allow us to see how these aggressive converts are competing with the older, established banks.

We checked out a few using the Internet (and we have listed their Web addresses in Appendix C).

Nationwide: Like the big four banks, the staunchly mutual Nationwide offers two different children's savings accounts. (For those of you who are mystified by the term 'mutual', you can look it up in Appendix B, otherwise known as the glossary.) The under-12s account, known as a *Smart 2 Save* account, currently pays gross interest of, wait for it, 6.95 per cent. And that beats the banks hands down.

All you need to open an account is £1. There's a 'Welcome Pack', which we know isn't important at all to Foolish parents and children, but at least you're not having to sacrifice a decent rate of interest in order to get it. There's the usual condition, too, that if the child is under seven, a parent has to handle the account.

Next comes the *Smart Account*, which is for children between the ages of 12 and 17. Same interest rate, same minimum opening balance of £1, but no welcome pack. You do get a cashpoint card though, and a *Smart Magazine*.

Halifax: The Halifax, which has converted to a bank, offers a *Young Savers* account, but with a current annual interest rate of just 4.25 per cent. And using the Halifax Web site, we couldn't find any more information on these accounts at all. So if you really need to know what pointless little gift, if any, your child will receive when the account is opened, then you'll have to call them and ask for yourself. But we bet you probably won't care too much. Not at 4.25 per cent gross per year.

And that 4.25 per cent interest is lower than the other three building societies we looked at, so the conversion to a bank hasn't been good news for young savers. So much for getting a little extra!

Alliance & Leicester: The Alliance & Leicester operates a *First Save* account for tiny investors. They don't bother with two different kinds of account for different age ranges. How sensible.

The Alliance & Leicester *First Save* account is currently paying an annual gross interest rate of 6.0 per cent, which is relatively respectable, and the usual £1 minimum opening balance applies.

Abbey National: Last but not necessarily least of the big names that we checked, the Abbey National has an *Action Saver* account for children aged under 16. Again, just one kind of account, not pointlessly split into two like so many. Mind you though, children under 12 do get to be members of the *Action Savers Club*!

And the interest rate? Currently 4.55 per cent gross, which is not the worst of the building society rates we have examined here, but not the stuff that millionaires are made of either.

There are plenty of other building societies around, of course, and we can't hope to cover them here. But our quick look at these four certainly suggests that the building societies offer greater potential for finding a better rate of interest than the high street banks, and that the mutual societies are likely to offer the best rates of the lot. All you need to do is shop around a little.

Long term? No thanks

Easy really. Well, we think it is anyway.

As a home for a Foolish child's long-term investments, an interest-bearing savings account just doesn't come close to being good enough. The best rate we have seen here, that from the Nationwide of a little under 7 per cent, is significantly below the average annual stock market return this century. And don't forget, that interest rate, effective as at the end of April 2000, comes after base interest rates have been hiked a few times too. When base rates fall again, as they almost inevitably will do, that 7 per cent will also fall. And if the UK ever approaches European base rates in an attempt to converge with the Euro, then savings account rates will undoubtedly fall even further.

Now, with an investment that offers a guaranteed annual return, we can't reasonably expect that return to be as high as the long-term return that is possible from investing in the stock market. The stock market, after all, doesn't offer any guarantees on a year-by-year basis. And the long-term average return from investing in shares might fall in the future, but there is still rather a large gap between the long-term returns from the two forms of investment. And those percentage points are what can make the difference between scraping by and living like royalty.

If you want to trust your children's long-term wealth to the banks and building societies, then we wish you the best of luck. But we're having none of it.

Short-term accumulation

But using a savings account for the short-term accumulation of money that will, when there's enough of it, be invested in the stock market in some form is very Foolish. So, who offers the best value?

Interest rates will change over time, of course, and so any new Foolish parent needs to have a look around and see what is currently being offered before making a choice. But it does appear that the high street banks just don't cut the mustard when it comes to offering decent interest rates, doesn't it? And they always seem to lag a bit behind some of the building societies, especially the mutual ones. The interest rate is not going to be quite so important for simple short-term accumulation of money, so the extra bit of interest that you may get from a special children's account is going to be of far less importance than it would be if you were considering using one for holding long-term investments. The children's accounts are intended to be controlled by the children themselves too, which may not be what you want at all, so it's probably best to make sure that you can control whichever type of account you choose.

Bear in mind, too, that instant access isn't really needed, because Fools aren't concerned with market timing. If you are saving regularly, then even a three-month delay in accessing the money seems reasonable if it gets you a better rate of interest. That means that you can plan to shift junior's money into shares up to four times a year, which will give you a good timescale over which to research each subsequent investment target.

And if your children need a piggy bank shaped like a safe, or a children's book or two, or a colourful stationery set, then go out and buy them yourself. Banks should be about investing your money and maximizing your returns. Get your books from a bookshop.

Chapter Seven: The stock market jungle

No other investment alternative rivals common stocks as a way of accumulating wealth. Unless you're flat broke, reading this from your death bed, and have no heirs, there will be a time in your life when it makes sense to hold common stocks.

Michael O'Higgins

Finally, we arrive at the Motley Fool's long-term investment choice: buying shares in good quality public companies on the developed world's stock markets.

When we mention the stock market, 'You've got to be joking!' might be your immediate reaction, 'It's my responsibility to safeguard my children's money, not gamble it away chasing hot share tips.' And you'd be right, gambling and 'hot share tips' couldn't be further from our minds when we talk about stock market investing. But it's a common reaction when people are first confronted with the suggestion that buying shares is a low-risk (when viewed long term) and highly rewarding approach to investment. Here's what Nigel Roberts (one of the first official UK Fools) had to say recently. . .

My wife and I are investing money for our daughter Catherine, and I have told many of our friends about what we are doing. It is amazing how often we get looks of amazement and even horror. People express the view that we are taking an unnecessary risk investing Catherine's savings into the stock market and that we should simply leave the money invested in a bank savings account.

But Nigel's no idiot, not by a long way, and he's not taking any unnecessary risks with his daughter's money.

The general fear that buying shares on the stock market is a hugely risky undertaking that mere mortals should steer clear of is understandable, though, and the mainstream press must take a lot of the blame for perpetrating such a notion. How often do we pick up a newspaper and read headlines like. . .

> *'FTSE reaches record high.'*
> *'Panic selling causes FTSE to fall 5 per cent.'*
> *'Internet companies continue to fly through the roof.'*
> *'£57 billion wiped off the value of UK shares.'*
> *'Regulators alarmed over high tech mania.'*
> *'19 charged in $8.4m insider trading case.'*

OK, we made up a few of those, but they're the sort of thing we read. The last three in the list, by the way, are actually genuine: two are from that august publication, the *Financial Times*, and one is from the BBC. This is just the kind of thing that the media prints. Why? Because their job is to sell newspapers, and boring 'It's fine, it's all right, nothing's wrong,' stories just don't sell.

So what is the truth, and why are people so scared of investing in shares?

1929 and all that

One of the first stock market scare stories that people encounter is the tale of the great 1929 crash. We've all heard of people's fortunes being wiped out overnight and stock brokers throwing themselves out of high windows, but how close to the truth is all that, and should we worry about it?

There are always bears about (and if you haven't come across the term 'bear' before, it is just a name given to people who think that the stock market is going to fall), and no matter how well the economy is performing or how modestly and sustainably the stock market is growing, there'll always be some of them telling you that a crash is just around the corner. Occasionally they're right, but not very often. And in between market falls, they'll be missing out on great long periods of impressive growth.

The bears will say things like, 'Anyone who invested in the US stock market at the peak of the 1929 bubble and held on through the crash would have lost 89 per cent of their money, and that's a catastrophe in anyone's language.' But if we think about it sensibly for a moment, we will quickly realize that things aren't quite like that in reality.

Firstly, stand up all of you who expect your children's investment career to consist of one large investment of all of their life savings, made on a single day, and then not a penny more for the rest of their lives.

Hmm, you're all still sitting down, we see.

Now, stand up everyone who expects their children's investments to be made little and often instead, possibly comprising regular monthly amounts, perhaps an irregular bit invested now and then, or maybe a combination of both.

Wow, what a crowd! OK, you can all sit down again, but not all at once – we don't want a tidal wave to hit China. If you were investing small amounts regularly in the late 1920s, and continued to do so over the bubble, into the crash and beyond, carrying on for another couple of decades, you wouldn't have done badly at all. You'd have beaten saving the money in the bank, that's for sure.

Take a look at the chart of the returns from UK shares since 1918. See how it starts way down on the left and ends high up on the right, turning an initial investment of £100 into £1 million. And see all those little wiggles along the way? Those are the crashes and crises that instil so much terror into so many people when you mention the stock market to them. You can hardly see them now, can you? And even the 1929 aberration doesn't look so scary when seen in a long-term light.

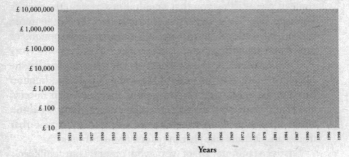

The truth is that for more than a century, the British stock market has outperformed all other forms of investment. And if you are looking to invest for decades, which is surely the case when you are considering investing for your children, then the short-term ups and downs really don't matter at all.

Oh, and before we leave the subject of stock market crashes – yes, some people did have their considerable wealth reduced to nothing in the 1929 crash. But the biggest culprit was margin trading. Margin trading means borrowing money to invest in shares, and a lot of people borrowed big. When the value of the shares you have bought with the borrowed money crashes, however, you can end up owing a lot more money than the fallen shares are now worth. So in 1929, bankruptcy prevented people from sitting back, continuing with their regular investments, and waiting for the recovery. The lesson is a simple one: don't invest on margin.

But if stock market crashes aren't as nasty as they are usually made out to be, are there any beasties that we should really steer clear of? Yes, there are.

Dangerous species number 1 (or Beware fund managers)

Amidst the vast fauna of investment species the genus *Cogniscentidae* (or 'The Wise') contains some of the most venomous, with several of their number being capable of inflicting quite serious injuries on the value of our investments.

One particular species, *Accipter maximus* (the 'Fund Manager'), following its ruthless Darwinian drive to dominate, has stopped at nothing in its attempts to steer other species away from investments that provide the best returns with the lowest charges and towards investments that enrich its own species instead, through high charges and commissions.

Adopting a similar tactic to *Cuculus canorus* (the 'Cuckoo'), the parasitic *Accipter maximus* will frequently expose its gaping craw to parents of other species who, thinking that they are satisfying the financial requirements of their own offspring, are only serving to fill the hungry gullet of the parasite instead.

Many individuals of this species have helped to create boot-quaking terror in us with their stories of stock market catastrophes, and of how we can't hope to win at that game because the professionals hold all the cards. They get all the insider information and all the latest hot tips first-hand from other species in their own order, you see, and can react to it, getting in and out, long before we private investors even get a sniff at it. And because of their privileged position, they will win and the small stock market gambler will lose. 'We have eyes and ears in every wine bar in the City,' they will claim, 'and we just love to make money for you.' So if we want to get ahead in the stock market, we'll need their professional guidance and their adept financial management. We shouldn't gamble our money buying shares for ourselves, but should invest our cash in their ably-managed investment funds instead. And that comes at a price, of course, and we'll have to pay their management charges and their commissions. But we can't expect such expertise to come cheap, can we?

But that is complete bunk, and they know it.

If professional fund managers are so good, then we should expect to see their managed investment funds soundly beat the market, year after year, should we not? Any old Tom, Wei Ling, or Mohammed can easily match the average market returns (and we'll tell you how you can achieve that yourself a little later) with little in the way of costs, so those steep management charges ought to bring us a significant bit extra.

But they don't. And we know that they don't. According to a survey carried out by Micropal in 1996, which compared the one-year, five-year, and ten-year performances of all UK unit trusts (and a unit trust is just a pooled, managed investment fund, of the kind that the Wise are supposed to be so good at running), only 15 out of a total of 203 unit trusts succeeded in beating the FTSE All Share Index (and don't worry about what that is exactly, as we'll be returning to the various stock market indices shortly). And to make it a fair comparison, the trusts' performances were measured with all dividend income re-invested and on an offer-to-bid basis.[1] That means that just 7.4 per cent of fund mangers managed to beat the index, with a whopping 92.6 per cent failing to match it. Since 1996, we have seen many claims that fund managers are improving their performance (perhaps some of them are doing it by following Motley Fool principles), though we won't actually start believing those claims until we see some proof in the shape of new improved long-term performance charts. And you know what? The evidence since 1996 actually suggests that they aren't improving as much as they'd like us to think at all.

1. The words 'offer' and 'bid' are part of the financial services lexicon, and are not particularly transparent terms at all. The 'offer' price is the price at which you can buy a share (or a 'unit' in a unit trust), and the 'bid' price is the price that you can sell it at. The price we usually see quoted for a share is something known as the 'mid-price', which is roughly half-way between the two. Measuring the performance of an investment by comparing the price that you sell at with the price that you buy at is the only fair way of doing it, and so Fools should beware of investments whose performance is advertised 'bid-to-bid' or using the mid-prices. If someone is selling an investment on anything other than an 'offer-to-bid' basis, they've got something to hide.

In fact, a survey carried out by The WM Company (which you can find at **www.index-tracking.co.uk** under the title of 'The WM Company Comparison of Passive and Active Management of Unit Trusts') discovered that between 1994 and 1998, 106 out of 114 actively managed unit trusts failed to match the index (after allowing for charges and the bid-offer spread). That's a 93 per cent failure rate, which is hardly a good advertisement for the industry.

Actively managed funds were also found to be more volatile during the period under study (that is, their values went up and down further, which is perhaps what we should expect from the more risky approach taken by an actively managed fund), but the more volatile ones actually put in the worst performances. So the extra risk taken by the highly paid managers actually came to nought. Less than nought, in fact.

But one of the most striking results of The WM Company's survey is that if you choose an actively managed unit trust on the basis of its previous five years' performance, one that is in the top quarter of the performance table, then the chance of that fund being in the top quarter over the next five years is no better than would be expected by pure chance. Hmm, when they add that statutory statement to their adverts that says, 'Past performance is no guide to future performance', they're absolutely spot on, aren't they?

Why do they underperform, long term? There are many reasons, but one that we should all remember is that fund managers have a very short-term focus for their investments. Their employers want to see their funds in the top ten best-performing funds at the end of the year, even though one year is hardly any time at all in investing. A fund manager who puts in a bad couple of years (by refusing to get carried away by the latest trend, for instance) will not hang on to his job for very long, even if he has a superior long-term strategy. That means that most of them are focused on short-term market timing and end up buying and selling far too frequently. This over-trading erodes our returns by putting the money into the pockets of brokers and market makers (and you can find out exactly what these are in Appendix B at the back) instead of into our accounts. And the result of this short-term focus? Some get lucky and make the top ten list; others don't. And we private investors should be sure not to confuse that luck with actual skill.

Think about all those pin-stripe suits, wide braces, and flashy sports cars that the City boys like to show off as macho symbols of their financial prowess. Someone has to pay for them. Do you really want that someone to be you?

Dangerous species number 2 (or Beware financial advisors)

No private investor should venture forth without being fore-warned of another particularly dangerous family, again of the genus *Cogniscentidae*. Perhaps the least dangerous, or at least the species with the poorest camouflage, is *Consultumpecuniae captivum* (the 'Tied Financial Advisor'). This particular species acts as a go-between, attempting to channel investors' funds towards its own employers. In such a position, this particular species of advisor is obliged to try to sell you its employer's investment products regardless of their value. If there are much better investments to be had elsewhere, then this particular advisor's eyes and ears are closed to them.

Tied (or dependent) financial advisors are actually obliged to state their position in their dealings with potential customers, and should point out that they can only recommend products provided by their employer. As mainstream investment products usually perform so poorly, and because your choice will be so limited, tied financial advisors are usually to be avoided when it comes to deciding on your children's investments.

A second species, of which there are two known varieties, is *Consultumpecuniae liberum* (the 'Independent Financial Advisor'). Of the two varieties, *Consultumpecuniae liberum v.*

mensarius (the 'Commission-based IFA') holds the most danger for your children's future wealth. This particular variety is paid by commission, and earns its entire income by taking a slice off the top of your investment (and it can sometimes be a surprisingly thick slice). To a lot of people, payment by commission may seem perfectly reasonable, and in many professions it may indeed be so. But in the world of investment such payment leads to an inevitable conflict of interest.

Suppose an 'independent' financial salesperson (sorry, we just can't handle calling them 'advisors' any more) has two different investment funds to sell. One of these has low charges of its own and has been performing reasonably well, though it pays only a small commission. The other carries steep management charges that hit its bottom line performance quite seriously, but it pays a handsome commission to the salesperson. Now, which of these investments do you think the salesperson is going to push you towards? How many of them would think, 'I'm going to advise my customers to put their children's money into the better-performing investment that doesn't pay me very much, and I will care nothing for the lucrative commission from the poorer investment that I'm passing up'? Conflict of interest? Certainly there is.

The second variety of this species, *Consultumpecuniae liberum v. chronologicus* (the 'Hourly Fee-Based IFA'), is a better bet for the astute long-term investor. This variety of salesperson charges for services by the hour and does not take any payments by commission. Some investment companies insist on paying a commission and will charge you as though you had paid it anyway, and so what these salespeople usually do in such circumstances is pass the commission back to you and send you a bill for their services. Or alternatively, they will take their fee out of the commission and pass the rest back to you.

So if you need financial advice, an independent financial advisor who charges by the hour and who does not accept enrichment in the form of commission is by far the best bet if you want to avoid becoming a victim of the conflicts of interest that riddle this profession. But do you really need financial advice in the first place? We think not, and that's what this book is all about.

Dangerous species number 3 (or Beware full service stockbrokers)

The last species that really isn't so good for your children's wealth is *Procuratus sumptuosum*, (the 'Full Service Stock-broker'). Long held in high regard, stockbrokers who offer advisory and management services in addition to executing your buy and sell orders have been falling out of favour in recent years. And it's about time too.

The services that such individuals offer range from advising you on what to buy and sell to taking control of your money and actually doing the buying and selling for you. And they make their hard-earned crust in the form of their commission on each deal. Fair enough, brokers deserve to make money from the work they do, just like everybody else, and commissions are far more reasonable than they used to be, thanks to fierce competition.

But wait a minute. If brokers make their money by taking a slice off the top of each trade you make, then the more trades you make, the more money they make, right? But the fewer trades you make, the less you lose in commissions to your broker. Beginning to see another conflict of interest? Remember those tables of compounded returns and the difference that just a couple of percentage points makes in the long term? Well, if you lose a couple of per cent by paying all those commissions to your broker for making too many trades on your account, then it is the broker who will be pocketing the long-term difference, not you.

The Motley Fool is a strong advocate of using an execution-only broker (one who just buys and sells what you want, offering no advice and taking no responsibility for your decisions at all), and buying good companies that you will want to hold for a very long time.

Who is the best manager?

It's time for a simple exercise now, and it consists of just one question. . .

'When it comes investing for their futures, who has the best interests of your children at heart?'

We'll give you half a minute to work out your answer, but we'd be surprised if it takes you more than a second or two. And if the answer doesn't come instantly to you, here are some possible candidates. . .

Is it going to be the fund manager who consistently under-performs the market and whose focus is on short-term annual results rather than long-term performance? No, of course it isn't.

Is it going to be those financial advisors who make their money from selling the products that pay the best commissions rather than those that provide the best performance for you? Not likely.

Is it going to be an advisory stockbroker whose rewards are driven by how frequently you buy and sell rather than how well your investments perform? Not in a million years.

Or is it that unpromising looking individual who stares back out at you from the bathroom mirror every morning? Yep, you got it, that's the one.

Nobody, absolutely nobody, is going to have your children's interest at heart quite like you have, are they? But you can't manage stock market investments yourself, surely? Even if you had the skill, you certainly don't have the time to spare to pore over all those numbers in the *Financial Times* every day and stay glued to each day's market news.

But you can do it, and it needn't take any real time at all. It is only decades of conditioning to the contrary by the Wise investing establishment that makes us think that we aren't worthy of such a task.

An investor not a gambler be

You don't want to lose everything? Just following a few simple guidelines should keep your kids' money safe, and destined to perform a lot better than it would in a bank account. In fact, you only really need to remember one simple principle to avoid those legendary wipe-outs, stories of which the newspapers love to scare us with: don't gamble, because gamblers lose, long term.

Don't try to time the market. Short-term trading and market timing are for mugs, not Fools. All those peaks and troughs on a company's share price chart look lovely with hindsight, don't they? And the Wise pundits and legions of chartists (or 'technical analysts' – people who believe that the only thing that matters is short-term movements in a company's share price) will point out that 'all you had to do was buy here, and sell there, and you'd have made 48 per cent in just three months.' Sounds good? Now take a blank piece of graph paper and a pencil, and ask the same pundits to draw in next year's price chart. Can they do it? No, of course they can't. And you can't either.

Don't follow tips. If you open the business section of any Sunday newspaper or any weekly investing magazine, you'll find a multitude of tips. There are so many of them, though, that there's no way you could hope to follow them all. And anyway, if you compare different publications and different 'experts', there's a good chance that they will disagree with each other. Let's look at a couple of examples, both taken from a UK investment magazine. . .

Example 1: '*Company 1* can be looked at as an income play with fantastic opportunities for growth. It is yielding just under 10 per cent, on a PE ratio of four. [. . .] A higher rate taxpayer can, at present, save around £300 a year in dividend yield.'

Example 2: 'When a company has a dividend yield of five times the FTSE All-Share average, a dividend cut is almost guaranteed. *Company 2*, the UK's third-biggest power producer and the company in question, has denied it will soon be forced to cut dividends. Analysts think otherwise. [. . .] Sell.'

You couldn't expect two more opposing viewpoints, could you? Company 1 was being suggested as a good one to tuck away in an ISA. It has an impressive dividend yield of 10 per cent (that is, a dividend equal in value to 10 per cent of the current share price), and your ISA will enable you to save the tax on that. And it has great growth prospects too. Yummy. But what is it? It's PowerGen. Company 2 though, we are told, hasn't got much hope of maintaining its high dividend and we should sell any shares we hold. But who is this company? Yes, you've probably guessed it. It's PowerGen again. They are both talking about the same company, and the two opposing tips were just six pages apart in the same magazine.

We're not saying there's anything wrong with differing opinions – you'll find plenty of them at the Motley Fool – but we do object to differing opinions that are presented as blanket recommendations. They don't encourage personal responsibility for investment decisions or a positive attitude towards learning.

Avoid emotion. Don't jump into an investment just because you've seen someone else making a killing on some great tip, or on the latest hot stock market sector, and you can't stand being left out. That's just greed, and it will be a long-term killer of wealth. A good few of today's high-flying Internet companies, for example, will amount to little in the long run, and there will be a lot of private investors who bought in just at the peak because the Internet 'is a sure fire thing and investments in it just can't go wrong.' But of course they can, and investing in a bad Internet company is just the same as investing in a bad company of any description. While the good ones will do very well, the bad ones will be firmly shaken out one day. It may be tomorrow, next month, or years in the future, but it will happen.

Avoid bandwagons. Don't put all your money on the latest investing craze (be it the Japanese market, or Australian mining companies, or Internet incubator companies, or whatever), particularly if it's something you don't understand (of which more later). That's a blind gamble; you're betting on the crowd being right and on something you don't understand coming good. Crowds are often wrong, particularly when the air is heady with the smell of lucre.

Don't borrow money to invest. Remember margin trading, which we mentioned when we were talking about the 1929 crash? That was one form of borrowing, and a disastrous one at that, for many investors. Borrowing money in any form to invest is just another gamble. You're betting on being able to achieve a better performance than the interest you are paying on the loan, and with the high cost of most loans these days, the odds are not as far in your favour as you'd need them to be. The cheapest personal loans at the moment cost around 8.5 per cent per year (with credit cards going up as far as 22 per cent and more). Now, stock market returns may have averaged 12.2 per cent a year since 1918, but the average return since 1869 has come in at 9.8 per cent, which is a lot closer to that personal loan rate. There have been periods when the average return was less than that, and there will be such periods again. In fact, there will be some years when the value of your investments will even fall (though the long-term investor will dismiss such years as irrelevant in the long-term march of time). Suppose you borrow money at 8.5 per cent. You'll need to make a return of at least that just to break even. But if you start with a few years of, say, 6 per cent per year, you will effectively be losing 2.5 per cent a year, and those few percentage points, particularly early on, make a big difference.

Be satisfied with good returns. Don't chase astronomical ones. If you follow the guidelines we have already looked at, you will probably have realized that if you chase astronomical returns, you'll be counting on a fair old dollop of Lady Luck falling neatly into the pot.

We have already seen that we don't need huge returns to put together a tidy fortune, just a few per cent above a bank savings account is all that's required. If the 20th century stock market returns repeat themselves in the future – and there's no convincing reason why they shouldn't – your child will have amassed quite a few shiny pennies by the time a few decades have gone by.

Let's finish this discussion by talking briefly about risk. Many people equate risk with gambling, thinking that if you make a high-risk investment, then you're simply taking more of a gamble. But in Foolish eyes, there is a distinct difference, and it comes down to how much you understand about the risk and whether you accept it. If you fully understand the investment you are making, and are completely happy with the level of risk you are taking – if it's right for your particular situation – then you are making a Foolish investment. If, however, you really have no way of evaluating your chosen investment's chance of success, but instead just have the feeling that although it seems very chancy, risky investments often provide the best reward and so what-the-hell-let's-go-for-it . . . well, then you're gambling.

A measured, fully understood, high-risk investment might be just the ticket for part of your child's investment holdings. But if you have understood the miracle of compound returns, and understand the investments that you are making, you'll know that investments like this should not form the bulk of the portfolio.

A Foolish conclusion

The title of this chapter might at first have filled you with a little trepidation. 'If the Motley Fool thinks that the stock market is a jungle, then what chance do we have?' you might have thought.

But now that you have finished the chapter (you did finish it, didn't you? We hope you didn't just skip straight to the end), you have seen that all the scare stories are just, well, stories, and they are designed to frighten you away and leave the lucrative investment business in the grasping hands of the Wise. And you have also seen how all those chisellers who try to chip away at your earnings over the years and pocket sizeable chunks of them for themselves are easily avoided by handling your investments yourself.

So now we hope you will agree with us that investing in the stock market isn't like hacking your way through an impenetrable jungle at all. No, it's more like a pleasant stroll through verdant summer meadows, or a quiet and reserved game of croquet on the lawn.

And when those around you are jumping on and off the latest bandwagons and filling their brokers' coffers with the commissions from their short-term trading, just sit back in the sun, keep nibbling at those cucumber sandwiches, and think about the pile that will have accumulated in a couple of decades to secure your children's future.

OK, time to move on and examine what options you actually have for investing your kids' legacies in the stock market.

Chapter Eight: But what should you invest in?

Each to his choice, and I rejoice.
Rudyard Kipling

Now we're getting to the crux of the book. In what exactly should you invest on behalf of your child? And we are talking shares, right? You are definitely convinced by now that shares are the best long-term investment for Junior. If you're not, go back and read Chapter Four again. We'll still be here when you get back.

If you asked a random selection of investors to describe their personal strategies for choosing companies in which to buy shares, the chances are that no two would have quite the same answer. Some would tell you that watching the news and the share price of a company, and diving in when the price falls and selling a short time after when it has risen again is the way to go.

You might also hear tales of technical analysis, day trading, margin trading (borrowing money from your broker to invest), futures, warrants, spread betting (gambling on the short movement of the stock market), and all sorts of other wondrous approaches. We talk about the first two of these in a little more detail further on, but none of these represent reliable long-term ways to increase the wealth of your children.

And you'll also hear people, known as fundamental analysts (and Warren Buffet, who we met earlier, is one of the best of this breed), who talk about finding good solid companies to invest in, ones that aren't going to go bust overnight; companies that you can buy shares in, then put the shares away somewhere and forget them. Now that approach is one that is close to our Foolish hearts, and we believe that long-term fundamental analysis is a safe, sure long-term strategy.

But there are all sorts of ways of looking at companies and not everyone will want to get involved with investing in individual ones. It's not that it's hard, but it does take a little time to learn about such things, and you need to think about the strategy that suits you best. One thing few parents have these days is much time, so if yours is limited, you might be interested in using one of a number of other simple and easy stock market investment strategies. We'll look at these before moving on to talk about individual shares. But first of all, let's answer one very popular question.

What about ISAs?

In recent years, the government has introduced Individual Savings Accounts (ISAs) in an attempt to persuade ordinary people to put a little bit by every year for their futures. Investments wrapped in ISAs are not liable for any kind of tax, whether on the income from dividends or on the capital growth in share prices, but can we use them to help our kids' investments?

Nope, we can't. ISAs are reserved for UK residents over the age of 18, so we can't use them for children. Tough, but there it is. Let's move on.

Index trackers

So you want to beat around 90 per cent of the professionals? Well, that's actually pretty easy. And you can do it in virtually no time at all.

Part of the reason why so many professionally managed

investment funds underperform the stock market average lies in the cut that the fund managers have to be paid. These fund managers are actually pretty expensive beasties, as their analysis and share picking takes time. Expensive time. The fact that they end up performing so poorly does, however, suggest that the money that they are being paid is not really being used to its maximum efficiency.

So, is there a simple mechanism for allocating all that pooled cash that investors have placed under managers' control? Perhaps one that can be done mainly by computers and which requires no human subjectivity or 'expertise'? And if there is, will this mechanism come close to matching the stock market average?

We'd hardly be asking all these questions if the answer was 'No', now, would we? The answer is that there is such a method and it's so easy that we can deduce it from first principles.

Think about a stock market index for a moment, say the FTSE 100 (see the section below, 'The FTSE indices'). If we could just buy shares in that whole index, instead of having to meticulously search for specific companies to invest in, we would beat most of the professionals, wouldn't we?

The FTSE indices

The companies quoted on the London Stock Exchange (the LSE) are listed in a number of different indices. Ignoring the Alternative Investment Market (AIM), the main indices are. . .

The FTSE 100 – the 100 largest companies by size

The FTSE 250 – the next 250 companies by size, after the FTSE 100

The FTSE 350 – the largest 350 companies by size, the FTSE 100 and the FTSE 250 put together

The FTSE All Share – The nine hundred or so companies listed on the LSE 'official list'.

To get some idea of the relative sizes of the companies listed in these indices, the FTSE 100, although it contains only one-ninth of the total number of companies in the FTSE All Share, currently accounts for around 80 per cent of the All Share index by value (though that will change over time as the relative valuations of companies change).

We could effectively buy shares in the FTSE 100 index by splitting our investment capital 100 ways, and investing a sliver of the appropriate size into each of those 100 companies. Thus, to a company which makes up 8 per cent of the FTSE 100, we allocate 8 per cent of our money, and to a company which accounts for 0.5 per cent of the FTSE 100 we allocate 0.5 per cent of our money, and so on.

Obviously, a private investor would have to be very well heeled indeed in order to follow such a strategy, or else they'd end up investing such small sums that it would be ridiculous. However, fund managers with millions of pounds of investors' money at their command can do it easily. And that is exactly what more and more investment companies are doing these days.

These 'Index Tracker' funds, as they are known, are becoming increasingly popular, and because they don't require expensive fund managers to keep them going, the charges for running them can be pared to the bone. In contrast to their humanoid counterparts, computerized fund managers, which are all that are needed to calculate the required spread of investment money over the companies in the index, require only a modest (and very cheap) supply of electrons and a wipe with a soft cloth every now and again. They certainly don't need a supply of expensive City lunches.

Because of this, index trackers typically charge around 0.5 per cent to 1.0 per cent of your investment per year, with no commission when you buy or when you sell. These are very low rates and in fact, at the Motley Fool, we would insist on never paying more than 1.0 per cent per year for an index tracker; and we certainly wouldn't be prepared to pay any other charges at all, especially an upfront commission which some other kinds of unit trust impose. In fact, we would set our Foolish limit on charges and terms pretty much in line with the government's 'CAT' mark guidelines. 'CAT' stands for 'Charges, Access, Terms' and represents value standards that the government thinks different types of investment should ideally offer. The exact details are unimportant; just reckon that an investment that conforms to 'CAT' standards is probably a good thing, at least as far as costs go. To qualify for a CAT mark, an investment fund must take no more than 1.0 per cent of the fund value per year in management charges, and must set a minimum lump sum investment amount of no more than £500, with a minimum monthly contribution of no more than £50 per month. Many index trackers actually have lower minimum amounts than this, and it is generally possible to invest as little as £20 per month.

The FTSE 100 isn't the only index, of course, and you can buy index trackers that follow other indices too. The FTSE 250, the FTSE 350, and the FTSE All-Share are all tracked, with the All Share being the most popular of these three. The FTSE All Share index, though, contains more than 900 companies, and trying to spread a chunk of investment money over such a large number of shares in proportion to their index weighting would be a daunting task. How such trackers work instead is by employing a representative sampling method. Rather than buying shares in every single company, the money is allocated to a number of companies selected by both market sector and size, and which are thought to constitute a realistic representation of the index. Such tracker funds might be expected to track their selected index less accurately, but most seem to do a decent job of it.

We can't list all the available index trackers here, and we can't recommend any specifically, because things change and we would probably be out of date by the time you read these words. And we really can't quote their charges, because they will change too. In fact, with the ever-increasing competition, charges are being cut all the time. So, you will need to do some research of your own, and be sure to shop around.

It doesn't actually make sense to compare the performance of a set of tracker funds, or at least, we shouldn't be looking for the ones that bring in a higher return than the index. In fact, if you find one that does, you should hear a warning alarm. This is because they all aim to match the index itself as closely as possible. Naturally, it's not always possible to mimic the index exactly, but any tracker fund that deviates significantly more than the others should be approached with caution. The things to compare, then, are the charges and the deviation of each tracker from the index itself. And if you are planning to make regular investments, the facilities offered for making such payments need to be compared too. You should never pay significantly more for the privilege of making regular monthly payments, so reject any companies that try to levy such a charge.

Any supplier of index trackers should be able to quote their tracking error. If they can't, then that suggests they aren't placing too much emphasis on measuring it, and so aren't as keen on keeping an eye on their performance as they should be.

What will an index tracker actually get you? Remember Chapter Three, when we examined the effect that compounding will have on your investments over a long period? Index trackers weren't actually around 60 years ago, but let's work out what you might have achieved with one, had it been available. What we'll do is assume that you invested £25 per month for 60 years. We'll also assume that your index tracker managed to match the historical 12.2 per cent annual return that the UK stock market has achieved since 1918, less 0.5 per cent per year in charges (we won't try to account for any index tracking error, as that should even out over the long term).

Sixty years in an index tracker at that rate would have got you just over £2 million, which wouldn't be a bad sum to put towards a comfortable retirement.

Doing the same using the 9.8 per cent that the stock market has returned since 1869, less that 0.5 per cent again, you'd have ended up with a noticeably smaller but still not inconsiderable sum of approximately £700,000.

We can't say, of course, what the long-term return from the stock market will be for the next 60 years. But we see no reason why it shouldn't stay comfortably ahead of banks, building societies, and all other types of investment.

Mechanical strategies

An index tracker should bring you roughly the average performance of the index you have chosen to track, less the management fees of 0.5 per cent to 1.0 per cent per year. It requires none of your time, and beats the great majority of professionally managed investments.

Now, that will probably be enough for most people, but can you do better without spending hours delving deep into stock market research? Well, yes, we think you can. In fact, the Motley Fool has developed a number of mechanical strategies that should take you just an hour or so every year. These strategies fall into two categories, Dividend Yield Strategies and Relative Strength strategies.

Dividend yield strategies. The Motley Fool's dividend yield strategies have been developed from the pioneering work done by Michael O'Higgins in his groundbreaking book *Beating The Dow*. O'Higgins spent some time studying the constituents of the American Dow Jones 30 index, which is an index of 30 hand-picked companies thought to provide a good representation of American business. The companies in the Dow Jones are all considered blue chip companies, and are favourite investments for older retired folk who rely on annual dividends paid to shareholders for their income. Those dividends, then, are pretty important, and the companies will do anything they can to avoid cutting them. Because of this,

O'Higgins wondered if he could use the dividend yield of these companies (and the dividend yield is just the dividend expressed as a percentage of the share price) to find ones with temporarily depressed share prices. He reasoned that if a company's share price was down (due to some short-term reason or other), then this would be shown by the actual dividend yield being unusually high. All of the 30 Dow Jones companies tend to pay similar dividends (as a percentage of their share prices) and so O'Higgins experimented with buying shares in the companies with the highest dividend yields and waiting for their share prices to recover (and those dividend yields to come down).

And he had a lot of success. What he did was to choose the ten companies in the Dow Jones with the highest dividend yields (implying lower than normal share prices), and then bought shares in the five cheapest, kept them for a year and then sold and redistributed the resulting money amongst the next 'Dow Dividend 5'. And why the cheapest? Because he reckoned that, for psychological reasons, investors were likely to buy back into nominally cheaper shares earlier than they would the more expensive ones.

At the Motley Fool, we did some back-testing of this strategy over more than thirty years and discovered that between 1961 and 1997, an investor following this 'Beat the Dow' strategy (as we like to call it) would have achieved an average annual return of 16.0 per cent, compared with the 12.1 per cent return from the Dow Jones index itself over the same period. Now, we already know what a difference four percentage points will make over the long term, but it might come as a surprise to hear that, while the Dow Jones provided a total compounded return over those 36 years of more than 6,700 per cent, the Beat the Dow strategy would have yielded almost 24,000 per cent.

How would this have worked with the FT-30, Britain's closest equivalent to the American Dow Jones index? Well, we tested it using data going back to 1983 (getting data from earlier than 1983 is quite difficult in the UK), and found an average return, up until the end of 1997, of 23.7 per cent. That would have turned an investment of £10,000 in 1983 into £243,000 by the end of 1997. Pretty good, eh?

We have been refining these strategies at the Fool of late, and on our UK Web site, over in the Foolish Workshop, we have been tracking some 'Beat the Footsie' portfolios (one starting every month and finishing 12 months later) for some time. We are currently using a simple strategy of buying the five shares with the highest dividend yields rather than factoring in the actual share prices, as O'Higgins did, because doing that really doesn't appear to be beneficial in the UK, according to our research.

But, we have to confess, our 'Beat The Footsie' portfolio (or 'BTF' for short), running since October 1997, is currently trailing the market indices (both the FT-30 and the FTSE 100). It has been suggested that a strong bull market (that is, a strongly rising market, such as we have been seeing for a few years now) is not good for dividend yield strategies, but we can't really tell if that is the reason. And it's still early days yet. Check out the Foolish Workshop on the Web site for the latest details, and for details of variations on the strategy.

Relative strength strategies. In the Foolish Workshop we have also been running some strategies based on something known as Relative Strength. Developed more recently, these are based on the observation that things that go up often tend to carry on going up further. The way to invest in one of these strategies is to take the five shares in the FTSE 100 that have risen the most over, say, the last six months, buy them and keep them for a year, and then sell them and buy the next five highest climbers. Oh, and we stick to the FTSE 100 to try to avoid buying complete rubbish that is just on a short-term boom-and-bust trip.

We have several similar strategies, the difference being the way the Relative Strength is calculated, and all are tracked on the Web site in the same manner that we track our 'Beat the Footsie' strategies. All are followed on a per-month basis – we buy the top shares and keep them for a year before selling.

Unlike our attempts to Beat the Footsie, our Relative Strength approach has been doing remarkably well recently, with some annual returns as high as 90 per cent. It is a strategy that is clearly more volatile than the BTF (which means it gives investors a rockier ride). Critics also suggest that it would only work in a bull market (a rising market, remember), and that a downturn (or 'bear' market) would cause havoc. That may be true, though we have not had a bear market through which to test it. And some would argue that, as we have far more rising years than falling years overall, we should still do fine providing we really are in it for the long term and can stomach the bad years that may come along from time to time.

As with the BTF, all of the latest standings and the variations on the strategy can be found in the Foolish Workshop on the Fool site. In addition, you'll find plenty of discussion about the strategies at the relevant discussion boards on the site. Check these out before making any investment decisions yourself.

Hand-picked companies

If index trackers don't provide a good enough return for you, and the idea of following mechanical strategies doesn't float your boat, then you will probably be thinking of playing a more active part in selecting the shares that you will buy for your children. And it really is a great way to do it. The chances are that, if you simply stick to buying large, well-known companies, you will do pretty well over the years. And you'll have no annual fees to pay that index tracker provider either, only the initial purchase and sale fees for the shares.

Different Foolish investors, of course, prefer different strategies. Some base their valuations on the estimates of companies' future earnings; some look for small growing companies and compare their expectations for growth with the current company valuations; others look for companies that are out of fashion and have fallen on short-term hard ground, hoping to buy cheap and hang on until the share prices recover; still others select individual sectors and learn all they can about them, restricting their investments to their chosen sectors.

Whatever your personal favourite strategy might turn out to be, describing and analyzing a large number of strategies is beyond the scope of this book. Countless other books have been written on the subject of investment strategies. (Modestly, we suggest the *Motley Fool UK Investment Guide*, which examines some of these strategies, and the *Motley Fool UK Investment Workbook*, which describes how to make sense of company accounts and valuation techniques, amongst other things.)

It is worth considering one approach here, though, and we can hark back to something that Nigel Roberts said about investing for his daughter: '*Once we have a reasonable sum built up in the account (say, about £1000), we buy shares for Catherine in blue chip companies, which we plan to tuck away and forget about until she comes of age.*' It is interesting that Nigel, who has considerable experience of investing in shares and whose speciality on the Fool Web site is writing about smaller capitalization growth companies, should choose blue chip companies for his daughter. Buy 'em and forget 'em, that's one strategy, and it's not a bad one at that. That's not to say you shouldn't be buying some more speculative shares with higher growth potential for your offspring as part of their overall portfolio, but a good foundation will be some shares in well-known, solid companies.

Blue chips

So what are they? Blue chip shares are shares in very large, prestigious, well-known companies. There is no hard and fast definition, but generally they are old established companies using traditional technologies and trading in stable market sectors. Big banks, some large telecommunications companies perhaps (yes, telecommunications is an old sector, even if it is going through a revolution at the moment), old established manufacturers and retailers, big oil and transport companies; many could be considered amongst the ranks of the blue chip brigade.

But where did we get the term 'blue chip' from? Ironically, it has its origins in gambling, which is one thing that investing in blue chip companies certainly isn't. Blue poker chips, you see, tend to be the high value ones.

The beauty of buying shares in blue chip companies is that you can, as Nigel does, just stash the shares away somewhere and forget about them, without having to look at them very often. The chances are that these companies will still be around and will still be doing fine in a couple of decades' time, and that your shares will have appreciated nicely in price. There's no guarantee, of course, as the record of Marks & Spencer has shown in recent years. (M&S would have featured on many people's lists of blue chip companies in years past, and was in fact featured in the Motley Fool UK Investment Guide.) But the occasional catastrophe shouldn't dent your total returns significantly if you have spread your kids' investment money across a number of companies, as you will see next.

Spreading the risk

At the Fool, we tend to think that a maximum of around ten to fifteen companies makes for a good-sized portfolio. Once you start getting much above ten companies, statistical analysis has shown that the lowering of your overall risk for each additional company shrinks very quickly, so the extra diversification serves no real useful purpose.

It's down to individual choice, of course, and some investors are happy to hold shares in dozens of companies. With large numbers of companies, though, it gets harder to keep a track of them all. And the more you stray from the big blue chips in your search for new investments, the more you will need to keep an eye on the fundamental performance of your companies.

Other investors prefer to hold fewer companies, going for a carefully focused portfolio rather than a diversified one, but overall, the Foolish suggestion of ten to fifteen companies is a good starting point.

Many of the constituents of the FTSE-100 could be considered to be blue chip companies, and if you use a strategy of buying shares in some of the biggest companies in that index, choosing different ones from different market sectors, you will be very likely to do just fine.

Some of the very best investments of the past have taken their place amongst the blue chips of today, and legends of these abound. When Coca-Cola, for example, was first floated back in 1919, one share of the company was priced at $40. A single share from that day, retained through all the years of growth and stock splits (the practice, when the price becomes uncomfortably high, of splitting a company's shares into a larger number of lower-priced shares, retaining the same total value of the company), would be worth something like $4 million today. Now that is a nice long-term investment.

Something similar has happened, albeit on a smaller scale, with a lot of the UK's blue chip companies, and the evidence suggests it's a phenomenon that is unlikely to stop any time soon.

For reasons of space, focus, and an editor breathing down our necks, we won't go into any more detail on strategies here and will refer you elsewhere (including to our Web site), but it is worth looking at a few strategies to avoid. Doing the right thing consists, at least partly, of avoiding doing the wrong things.

Strategies to avoid

We mentioned a few duff strategies in the introduction to this chapter (well, we think they're duff anyway; certainly as far as long-term investing for kids goes), and we'll have a look at three popular ones here.

Technical analysis. Technical analysts effectively base their strategies on the expectation that everything that is known about a company at any one moment is reflected in the share price. They carefully examine share price charts, fitting the share price movements to patterns that they think they recognize from the past and, using the belief that those patterns will happen again, attempt to predict where the share price will go next. If you listen to them, you will hear talk of all sorts of patterns, from the 'head and shoulders' to the 'double bottom' to the 'triple somersault with half pike' (OK, we made up the last one). Many investors swear by this approach, and good luck to them, because we think they'll need it. Most Fools, though, would put technical analysis in the same drawer as tarot cards and entrail-reading. There is no logical connection, as far as we can see, between yesterday's share price, today's share price, and where it's going to go tomorrow. And technical analysis is a time-consuming short-term strategy anyway; not much use to a hard-pressed new parent, even if it did work.

Day trading. A popular new phenomenon, encouraged by the growth of the Internet and the availability of cheap online stockbrokers, day trading is the stuff of modern legend. These day traders, buying and selling on the peaks and troughs of share prices during the day, and very rarely holding any shares overnight, are rumoured to be making millions. But several recent surveys in the USA, where day trading is at its most popular, concluded that the majority of day traders are using strategies that will ultimately lose them all their money. A common conclusion is that they need to make an annual return of something like 60 per cent just to cover their costs and break even. So to match the average stock market return of 12.2 per cent since 1918, they need to make 72.2 per cent; and to justify all the time they spend, the extra risk they take, and the coronary heart disease that they are surely setting themselves up for, they really need a return significantly better than that.

Penny shares. One of the first traps that many investment beginners fall into is buying penny shares. They're cheap, goes the argument, so you don't need much money to invest in them. And a share priced at, say 5p, will have a lot more potential than one that has already reached £5, and it can't fall very far. And people are convinced. But it is all complete nonsense. Firstly, the absolute price of a company share is completely meaningless, and should only be used in the context of the total valuation of a company. 100 shares priced at 5p each, for example, are worth exactly the same amount as a single share at £5. Two otherwise identical companies, one with its shares priced at 5p and one with its shares priced at £5, will have the same future prospects; it's just that the first company will have 100 times as many shares in circulation. And as for the bit about penny shares not having as far to fall – remember that every investment, no matter what the actual share price, can potentially lead you to exactly the same loss: 100 per cent. A £1,000 investment in shares that are originally priced at 5p and which then fall to 2.5p will lose you exactly the same money as a £1,000 investment in shares priced at £5 which subsequently fall to £2.50. Penny shares tend to have much bigger percentage spreads, too (that is, the difference between the price that you can buy at and the price that you can sell at), and so you will end up paying more in commissions. And finally, companies don't often float at penny share prices; it usually takes years of poor performance to get there. Penny shares frequently represent companies on their way down, and they often keep going in that direction.

Buy what you know

Before we leave this chapter, let's spare a thought for one of the oldest bits of investing advice in the book. 'Buy what you know' is one of the most oft-quoted investment maxims, but it is also one of the most misunderstood. And that is because it is so frequently followed without qualification. Here are a few fictitious quotes of the kind that we tend to hear from time to time. . .

'I bought shares in MFI a couple of years ago, because I know the furniture business.'

'I really like fancy ties and socks with cartoon characters on, so I'll buy shares in Tie Rack and Sock Shop.'

'I've spent thirty years as a travel agent, so I'm buying some Airtours shares.'

'I'll have some Marks & Spencer shares because I know a thing or two about knickers.'

Some of these examples might actually be decent long-term investments (though a couple of them don't seem to be doing too well at the moment). But those are lousy reasons for buying them.

'Buy what you know' doesn't mean, 'Buy companies in the business you work in, regardless of how bad that industry's health is.' And it also doesn't mean, 'Buy what you know even if what you know is rubbish.' But that's what some people end up doing.

No, what it means is that we shouldn't make an investment that we don't understand. We shouldn't invest without doing our homework first. Fancy MFI? Subject their last five years' accounts to a bit of scrutiny and see how their sales have been doing. Do a few simple sums and see if their profit margins are increasing or decreasing. Go and have a wander around furniture showrooms and see how busy they are compared to their competitors, and check how their prices and quality compare to those competitors too. And if they don't look like a good investment, walk away and look somewhere else, even if you are Professor of Flat-Pack Furniture at the University of

Wallamaloo. Remember, a bad investment doesn't suddenly turn into a good one just because you happen to work in the same industry.

So whenever you hear the phrase 'Buy what you know,' you might be better off thinking of it as 'Don't buy what you don't know,' or perhaps even better, 'Know what you buy.'

Onwards

This has been a very basic summary of different types of share-based investments that you might like to invest in on behalf of your children. Unless you're going to be investing in an index tracker – which is a very reasonable option – you should probably go elsewhere for more information, either from some of our other books, or from our Web site. Hopefully, however, it has covered some of the most basic things you need to know. All we need to do now is put it all together and get those pennies rolling into those long-term investments. And that's where we're headed next.

Chapter Nine: Putting It All Together

When we build, let us think that we build forever.
John Ruskin

Shares, that's what we want, possibly in an index tracker. But if we're going for shares in hand-picked companies, then it will be good quality companies that we are looking for, ones that we think may still be around and doing well in 30 or 40 (even 50 or 60) years' time. And to save our money in the short term until we have enough for a share purchase (or for buying extra units in that index tracker fund), we need a deposit account of some sort. We also need to make sure we do the right things regarding our children's ownership of their money, and be sure to handle taxation matters properly.

So that's what this chapter is about: putting it all together and making sure we jump through the right hoops and tie up all the red tape properly.

But before we go through the individual steps, let's go over to Nigel Roberts again (remember, the Fool we met earlier, who has been investing for his daughter Catherine since she was born, and whose friends tend to be a bit surprised to hear he is investing her money in shares). Here's what he had to say recently about how he handles it. . .

'When Catherine was born, she was given a number of cash presents by family and friends. We saved this money for her, resisting the temptation to run out and buy nappies with it. We also plan to save the child allowance that the government so kindly gives to us and any additional cash

presents that she is given. Over the next 18 years, we hope that this will grow into a sizeable sum that will set her up for the rest of her life.

'We opened a building society account for Catherine, into which we pay all the money. The account was opened in our names but designated Catherine as the beneficiary. This means that while we have control of the account, the money is treated as hers, and she will be able to take control of it when she reaches 18.

'When we opened the account, we completed the R85 Inland Revenue form given to us by the building society so that any interest is paid gross. Parents should be careful here – if you make a gift to your child that earns the child income of more than £100 in any one tax year, the whole amount will count as your own income for tax purposes. With two parents, there is a £200 limit. This rule only applies to gifts from parents, not other relatives or friends, and on money given from other sources children have the same income tax allowance as adults.

'Once we have a reasonable sum built up in the account (say, about £1000), we buy shares for Catherine in blue chip companies, which we plan to tuck away and forget about until she comes of age. If you are investing money for your children we would strongly recommend that you adopt a long-term strategy and be willing to tuck the money away for a minimum of five years – preferably much longer.

'If you are buying shares for your child (or unit trusts, for that matter), you buy them in your name. Normally you add the child's initials after yours to designate that the shares are held on your child's behalf. For example, in our case, the shares are held in the name NG and BB Roberts (CSR). The "CSR" indicates that we are the registered owners of the shares or units but Catherine Sheree Roberts is the beneficial owner. This is known as a 'bare trust,' is easy to set up and needs no involvement from a solicitor. As parents we act as bare trustees, looking after the investment on behalf of the *child until the shares (or units) can be registered in the child's name. This will be when she reaches 18 (16 in Scotland) and we as trustees are obliged to hand over the assets of the trust.'*

That is a pretty good summary of how to go about it, and we will now look at the individual steps that Nigel has taken. The most important is the establishment of a 'bare trust'. A bare trust is a very useful tool for Fools, and we will be covering such beasts in some detail shortly. But first, let's get a few tax considerations out of the way.

Taxing matters

Taxation can be a complicated thing, and the rules can and do change regularly. The information that we are offering here could easily be out of date now that you have the book in front of you, and there may be individual circumstances surrounding your own investments that require different treatment. So really, we offer these words just as a guideline. You should always check things out with your local tax office, and if you have any uncertainties regarding your own circumstances, you may be well advised to consult a professional tax advisor.

Children have the same annual income and capital gains allowances as adults (but see 'Bare Trusts', below, for a special exception), and exploiting these efficiently will go a long way towards maximizing your children's long-term wealth. You don't want money that you have saved for your children falling foul of your own personal taxation limits, after all.

So, income tax on interest first. When you open any interest-bearing account for your children, be it with a bank or building society, and whether it is a savings account or a stockbroker's cash account, get hold of and fill in form R85. That will enable interest on the account to be paid free of tax, whereas without it, tax at the basic rate will be deducted from the interest before it is paid. You should be able to get a copy of form R85 from the bank or building society branch where you opened your account, but if you can't get one there, any Inland Revenue office can send you one.

You need to fill in the details of your child's savings account and permanent address. If the child is over 16 and has been in employment at any time during the previous three years, then you will also need to enter his or her National Insurance number. For children under the age of 16, you need to sign the form on their behalf. Once past their 16th birthday, they can sign such forms for themselves.

Leaflet IR110, *A guide for people with savings*, is probably worth having a look at too. Again, you should be able to get this from any Inland Revenue office, but you can get it a lot easier from the Inland Revenue Web site (**www.inlandrevenue. gov.uk**). The site is a pretty comprehensive one, and offers an assortment of forms and leaflets for downloading.

The current single person's annual income tax allowance, for the year 2000-2001, is set at £4,385, and the annual capital gains tax threshold (the amount you can earn before paying CGT) is currently set at £7,200. With one exception (the £100 that Nigel mentioned above) that we will look at in some detail below, each of your children can earn these amounts of money from income and capital gains respectively before becoming liable for any tax. If a child does make any taxable income or capital gains, then they must be declared to the Inland Revenue using a standard tax return. Tax returns are not normally sent to children, of course, so it is your responsibility to request one and ensure it's submitted correctly.

Which savings account?

When you open a savings account for a child, the two big things that you should consider are its interest rate, and whether you can maintain control of the money in the account, as we discussed back in Chapter Six. Forget all the silly gifts (we looked at those earlier, too) and just go for the best deal. And remember, the chances are that you are going to get a better deal from a building society than from a high street bank at the moment – in our experience anyway.

Once you've decided where you're going to open the account, you still have a couple of options. You can open one of the accounts are aimed at children themselves, allowing the money to be held in your child's own name according to the regulations of the bank or building society involved; or you can open an account in your own name, with your child named as the beneficiary (using the 'bare trust' method described below), passing over the control of the money to the child when that 18th birthday arrives.

Whether you can open one of the special children's accounts in your name as a bare trust, without losing the preferential interest rates that they offer to children, depends on the individual bank or building society (though one, the Alliance & Leicester, certainly advertises this possibility). This kind of account, of course, is aimed at encouraging children to use the accounts for themselves. You may have to forego that extra bit of interest in order to maintain your control via a bare trust, and you may be just as well off opening an ordinary account rather than bothering with a children's account at all. If you are going to be accumulating money fairly quickly and regularly, then the interest rate is not going to make any real difference over the short term anyway.

Whichever way you choose, it is important to establish that the child is the beneficiary of the money that you invest. If you simply keep the money (and the stock market investments that you make) in your own name, with the intention of handing over a whole sackful of the stuff as an 18th birthday present, then you may be hit with taxation problems (and again, we'll talk about these particular problems later). If you have been investing well, then those 18 years of investments will have grown to a tidy sum, and you don't want the Inland Revenue getting their hands on any more of it than is absolutely necessary.

Now, what are you going to save in this account? Birthday presents, Christmas presents, Child Allowance, they're all candidates for popping into your children's savings accounts, together with your own regular or irregular contributions. Or just any other spare bits of money that you have left over from time to time.

Bare trusts

So, you want to hold investments (cash, shares, etc) with your children as beneficiaries, and you want to keep control of those investments until the children are old enough to shoulder the responsibility themselves. But you also want the investments to be assessed under your children's tax allowances, not your own.

And that's where the idea of a 'bare trust' comes in. It's a simple device that achieves exactly the above, and which doesn't cost anything at all to set up (if you really want to splash out and register your bare trust with the Inland Revenue, you will have to stump up 50p, but that is entirely optional). And it is applicable to bank accounts, building society accounts, stockbroker accounts, the lot.

These days, some application forms for savings accounts and brokers accounts have a box on them for you to specify the beneficiary of the account (and in fact, an increasing number of investment companies operating index trackers include this option on their forms too). If such a box is there, you can use it to designate your child as the beneficiary, and that will effectively create a bare trust for you.

But you can still open a bare trust even if there isn't a box like this. All that is required is for the account to be opened in the adult's name (or jointly, in two adults' names if you want), with the child's initials added in parentheses afterwards. So the account name might look something like these examples. . .

'Gomez & Morticia Addams (WA)'

'Homer Simpson (BS)'

'Marge Simpson (LS)'
'NG and BB Roberts (CSR)'

You might like to know that the account holder and the beneficiary don't have to be related – any adult can create a bare trust for any child.

And also note that if you want to invest money for two or more children, you will need to set up a separate bare trust for each of them. You can't create a single bare trust to cover all your children – the practicalities of who owns how much of it, which portions of each child's tax allowance should be used, how much each of them will get at age 18, and so on, would all conspire to make it impossible to administer. So it has to be one for each child.

Bare trusts in this form are very basic but are legally binding, even though they need no costly solicitors or other professionals to create or administer. The 'trustees' of the account are the named adults, and the investments held within the trust become the child's direct property at the age of 18. The trustees then no longer have any control over it.

Throughout the life of the trust, the trustees can actually do anything they want with the money (using the account to launder drug money, though, would be transgressing a few other laws, and really isn't advisable). It's possible that the Inland Revenue might take an interest if it looks as though you're using a bare trust to protect some of your own capital from taxation (and that is a little bit on the illegal side). The Inland Revenue, in fact, has the power to investigate any suspected attempts at tax evasion, and the penalties for being caught red-handed are pretty severe. Legally minimizing your tax bill is a sensible cornerstone of a long-term investing approach, but tax evasion is another matter altogether, and one that stands a good chance of leading to ruin instead of riches. Avoid it and sleep well.

Bare trusts actually offer the child no protection from irresponsible parents (but then, if you're irresponsible, you're probably not reading this anyway and care little for your children's future). This is a pretty simple logical deduction given that the trustees have control of the money. So, a bare trust is intended as a means for honest parents (and other adults) to invest money for children in such a way that income and gains from it are not subject to taxation at adult tax rates, and so that no unpleasant complications like inheritance tax can touch it if you're unfortunate enough to pop your clogs early (though we hope you don't, of course). It also keeps their grubby little paws off the dosh until they're 18, so they can't use it to set themselves up as playground loan sharks, Pokémon card brokers, or whatever else their fevered imaginations may come up with.

How do you go about registering a bare trust with the Inland Revenue? Just contact any tax office and ask them how to create a *declaration of trust*. Some investment companies will be able to help too, so you might want to try calling your tracker provider instead. Once you have completed your declaration, you simply send it back to the Inland Revenue enclosing the fee (which was 50p when we checked). There really does appear to be no advantage to registering a bare trust with the Inland Revenue, but some people still prefer to do so, and there's nothing to lose apart from that 50p if you do. But remember that an extra 50p lump sum invested at 9.8 per cent per year will amount to a grand total of £2.69 in 18 years' time!

Now, on to that tax allowance limitation, the £100 per year we mentioned earlier. Children are entitled, as we said, to the same standard allowances for income tax and capital gains tax as adults. And that applies to gains derived from whatever capital they have accumulated through gifts, etc. But tax-free gifts from parents are limited (even if gifts from any other benefactors are not). The limit to the amount of money given by parents is based on the income derived from that money, and that means interest or share dividends, not capital gains.

If the income generated in any one year from gifts given by any one parent amounts to more than £100, then the whole of that income is treated as if it is the parent's income, and will be taxed according to the parent's tax bands and allowances. For two parents, the total annual tax-free income rises to £200. Oh, and don't forget, as the money is deemed to belong to the parent for tax purposes (even if the child is the bare trust's named beneficiary), then it is the parent's tax return on which it must be declared.

And beware; this applies to the total income earned in any one year from *all* accumulated gifts from parents (i.e., accumulated over previous years). So if the child earns more than £100 in any one year from parental gifts given over the child's lifetime, then that income is taxed at the parent's marginal rate.

Now, one regular contribution that many parents make is the money that the government kindly contributes in the form of Child Allowance. Given to parents of all children up until the age of 16, and currently coming in at £60 per month, this adds up to a tidy sum over those 16 years. But be careful of the tax implications. Child Allowance is considered as having been paid to one or both of the child's parents, usually the mother; and it counts as a gift when it is paid into the child's account. Because of that, it will be subject to the £100 income limit.

Gifts from other people are not subject to this limit, and grandparents, uncles, aunts, friends, or whoever, can give your children as much as they want without worrying. It is only parents who get stung.

You may wonder why this limit is there at all. If other people can give your kids whatever gifts they want without worrying about tax, then why can't parents be similarly generous without having to pay through the nose for the privilege? Quite simply, it's an attempt to stop parents using their children as a tax dodge. If unlimited gifts were allowed, then unscrupulous people could invest a whole load of their money in their children's names and use up their children's income tax allowance in addition to their own (not to mention another helping of that capital gains allowance), taking the cash back sometime later. Like many well-meaning regulations, this one does seem to punish honest parents to prevent dishonest ones from cheating the Inland Revenue.

But how much damage does this parental gift limit actually do to a child's investment returns? Remember that it is only income that this limit applies to, so capital gains can be ignored. Now, assuming that our investments are in the stock market in one form or another, then it is dividend income that derives from shares that we are talking about. Using an index tracker as an example, let us assume an annual dividend payment of 2 per cent, which is close to the stock market's long-term average.

To keep our dividend payments below that crucial £100 per parent per year then, or £200 in total (assuming there are two parents), we are looking at total parental gifts of £10,000. Using our long-term examples of parents paying £25 per month into an index tracker for each child, and assuming that each parent is deemed to be contributing half, it would take 33 years to reach the limit; so that shouldn't be much of a problem.

And even if you are contributing £100 per month between you to your child's investments, it will still take eight years and four months to reach the limit. After that, you will be paying tax on all of the dividend income in each year in which it exceeds £100 per parent. For every £200 of dividend income, then, if both parents are higher rate taxpayers (currently 40 per cent), the Inland Revenue will take £80 from you in tax. But the compounding growth in the value of the shares belongs to the child and, provided the annual capital gains tax exemption limit hasn't been exceeded, no tax should be payable on that.

So, in most cases, the tax savings on the long-term growth in the value of your children's shares should far outweigh any income tax that you might have to pay. And if you kept the investment in some other form in your own name, you'd pay tax on the income from it in any case.

You may worry about your children receiving a single (large) capital gains tax bill when, at the age of 18, they take control of their investments and decide to sell the lot. There are a few things that can help to alleviate such a hit. First, if you've been buying hand-picked shares yourself, you may well have offset a lot of the capital gains over the years by selling some shares to buy others, and so consolidating the gain against your child's allowance for the year in which the shares were sold.

And if you have never actually sold any of your children's shares and so have not realized any actual gains while they were tax free, the shares will be subject to taper relief on any capital gains tax liability. For a higher rate taxpayer, for example, the disposal of any shares held for ten years or more will be liable to capital gains tax of only 24 per cent rather than the usual 40 per cent (that is, using the currently applicable taper relief figures; the chances of chancellors keeping their tweaking little fingers off them until today's new babies need to worry about them seems very slim indeed. So again, you should check for yourself).

And anyway, if you have educated your children Foolishly, then they won't want to cash it in and blow the lot, will they? No, instead they'll want to keep adding to their piles, and managing their own investments for themselves. They'll have many happy years to come, in which they can exploit their annual capital gains allowances for themselves.

Other trusts

A number people have asked us, on the Motley Fool discussion boards, how they can hold investments in trust for their children until later than their 18th birthday. Many people, thinking back to their own mis-spent youths, don't think that the little blighters will be trustworthy enough at that tender age, and will quickly spend the lot. Some people want the cash held until they're 21, others until they're 35, or whatever.

To set up any other kind of trust requires the use of professional legal services, and could run to a few quid. There are so many different legal ways of implementing such things, and so much depends on your own personal circumstances and requirements, that there really isn't anything that we can offer within the scope of this book. Such services are available, but you will need to seek legal advice if that is really the path you wish to tread.

And preventing your kids from misusing their investments is a great incentive to making sure that they are Foolishly educated in the first place, don't you think?

Hold it yourself

Another question that is sometimes asked on the discussion boards concerns holding your children's investments in your own name until you feel they are sufficiently able to take over themselves. There's nothing to stop you from doing this, but it could cost a fair bit in lost tax allowances.

Any money that you invest in your own name with the intention of transferring it to your children in the future will be subject to your own income and capital gains tax allowances. If you are using these to the full for your own income and investments, then any income and capital gains made on the kids' portion of your investment will be taxed at your marginal rate (up to 40 per cent for a higher rate taxpayer).

And if you should kick the bucket before you get round to handing it over, then it will all form part of your estate, distributed according to your will, and will be subject to assessment for Inheritance Tax. And even if you stay alive until you have handed it over, you'll still need to ensure that you keep breathing for another seven years. Because, if you expire before seven years are up, then that gift will be treated as an inheritance anyway, and Inheritance Tax will raise its ugly head again.

So it's really not worth it. Set up a bare trust, that's what most Fools would recommend.

Pegging out

That last thought, about making sure your children's investments don't get stung by Inheritance Tax, brings us to one last thought for this section. Make a will. Go on, do it right now. Dying intestate (that means without a will, in case you were wondering) can create all sorts of complications for your offspring; complications they really will be better off avoiding. If you croak while they are still young, this will be unpleasant enough for your children without you compounding their anguish by making the inheritance procedure a mess.

Now, with that cheery thought over, let's move on from concentrating on how to turn our children into wealthy young adults, and start thinking about how to turn them into Foolish young adults too. That is the subject of the next section.

Chapter Ten: School blues

The founding fathers in their wisdom decided that children were an unnatural strain on parents. So they provided jails called schools, equipped with tortures called education. School is where you go between when your parents can't take you and industry can't take you.
John Updike

OK, time for a quick reader survey. Hands up all those who learned anything useful about personal finance, or money management, or investment while at school. Hmm, thought not. Personal finance and investing has just never been on the official school curriculum and that's a problem.

Quite why that should be so is a bit of a mystery. Perhaps it's historical: it's only recently that people leaving school could ever expect to have more than a couple of farthings to rub together. Maybe it's a hangover from that antiquated view of life: school, followed by pit or factory, then retirement, then the grave. Or maybe it is just a remnant of the old Victorian British view that money is too vulgar to discuss. Who knows?

Whatever the reason, the fact is that our schools today generally show a lamentable and utter disregard for teaching the one subject that every single pupil is guaranteed to need throughout his or her life. It doesn't matter what academic subjects a child might favour, or which career path will finally be chosen; we live in a capitalist society, and everyone will need to handle the folding stuff. Understand money, and you understand the basic threads binding together modern society.

A Fool's schooldays

My school was a pretty academic one, and when it came to academic subjects, it did a fine job. It did well enough to get me off to university fired up with enthusiasm, which is what academic schools are all about, really.

To this day, I can still remember those chemistry lessons – those practical demonstrations of the pyrotechnics that you can get from a few innocent-looking bottles of strange coloured powder; and the clouds of thick choking smoke that often used to accompany them. Those exciting demonstrations were a kind of release, cleverly timed escapes in between periods of hard learning. If we learned all about spin-orbit coupling, understood that Erwin Schrödinger didn't actually have a cat, and showed that we cared about it all, we got those fiery demonstrations as a kind of reward.

In history too, a subject that I really didn't like much, I'll never forget one teacher who always used to punctuate the boring stuff with re-enactments of famous battles – in the classroom, with desks piled up as hills, or as ships. It would probably fall foul of modern safety regulations (as would those chemistry demonstrations), but we loved it and it certainly helped me to learn stuff that I wouldn't otherwise have been interested in.

But I never learned the first thing about money.

Sure, there were practical subjects like woodwork and metalwork, and they were fun too. I made an inlaid chessboard out of two different coloured woods once, and mounted it on a table. The corners of the squares even lined up (almost). That old table is still lying around somewhere, with a potted plant on it, probably. But just how often have I needed such a skill in later life?

It would have been useful to have really understood the wealth-making power of compound returns, though.

Metalwork was the same. Those name tags and coat hooks and the like were fun to make, but I've never needed to make anything of the sort since.

Oh, if only I'd learned something about the stock market instead.

What do kids want?

An episode of BBC 2's *Working Lunch*, early in April 2000, revealed the results of a survey of schoolchildren. The survey asked schoolchildren of different ages what they thought of their schools and how they should be improved, and one of the questions put to the kids was what extra subjects they would like to be taught at school. And the most popular answer, by quite a long way, was money management. A full 48 per cent of the children questioned put personal finance at the top of the list.

We, as Fools, are painfully aware of the need for financial education. Our children appear to understand the importance of such education too (and actually want to get some of it), but what about the government?

Well, there doesn't seem to be much prospect of getting personal finance included in the school curriculum any time soon. A large part of the problem is that schools, whatever the claims of politicians or academics, are not focused on helping to equip young people for their adult lives. No, they are focused on getting kids to pass exams. In fact, it would be very surprising indeed if schools were to take any other approach when their own success is measured by their examination pass rates. They'd be crazy to do so.

Where does it fit?

Fitting personal finance and investment into existing curriculum subjects relies on tenuous links, to say the least. Some people try to get personal finance included in economics. But really! Did anyone out there ever do economics at school? Let's turn to an economics textbook that just happens to be lying around and see what subjects it covers. Let's see, yes, here are a few. . .

Elasticity and Consumers' Surplus
Applications of Price Theory
Indifference-Preference Theory
Macroeconomic Concepts and Variables
Fiscal Policy
Monetary Policy

Do any of those sound like they've got anything at all to do with personal finance, or with investment? No, of course not, because economics (at least as taught in academia, and as tested by examination) is about as far away from the practicalities of personal investment as New Zealand is from Novia Scotia. Oh, and do any of those subjects sound exciting, the way learning how to become a millionaire might sound? Nope. And any suggestion that only economics students need to understand personal investment would obviously be silly.

How about another favourite: mathematics? It's in maths lessons that most children learn about compound returns. But it always seems to be presented in such a dull, dull fashion. Has any maths teacher, anywhere, ever tried to teach kids about compounding by pointing out just how wealthy they could make themselves if they invested a little money at a decent rate of return and left it there for a reasonable length of time? Hmm, we don't see anyone jumping up and shouting 'Yes, yes, that's exactly what my teacher did.' If it were taught like that, though, the idea just might stick, and a little bit of enthusiasm just might be generated. And, hey, if mock battles could prove so memorable for a young schoolboy who hated history (see 'A Fool's Schooldays' above), then think what something similar on the subject of money might do.

But no, whenever compound interest is taught (and it is taught specifically as 'interest'), it always seems to be presented as a debt calculation. 'Suppose you borrow X pounds for Y years at Z per cent per year. How much will you have to pay back in total?' That's the kind of stuff they teach. And 'Wow, that's a lot of money to pay back. Compounding bad: avoid compounding,' is the kind of thinking it's likely to create in young minds. Instead of instilling into young people what a great thing compounding is when they put it to their own use, they teach them what a nasty thing it is because it will make their loans cost so much more.

And investment isn't only for maths students either.

Another favourite. How about business studies? That's a subject that is growing in popularity these days (which in itself is no bad thing). But what have company finance, or floating a public company, or accounting regulations, or industrial relations laws got to do with investing your own private money for your own long-term financial security? Not a lot.

And why should personal finance education be solely the reserve of business studies students? If personal finance, money management, or investment (or whatever you want to call it) is to be taught as part of an existing school subject, then it really has to be something that is aimed at all pupils; something that isn't restricted to any specific discipline or particular academic ability.

This brings us to the last of the subjects in which financial education is covered, and that is the modern, trendy-sounding subject of personal & social education, or PSE (sometimes referred to as PSD – personal & social development). This is a subject that really is aimed at providing genuinely needed 'citizenship' style skills, and getting the most out of life in a capitalist society surely requires the skills of handling money and planning investments.

But how many schools actually teach anything about investment as part of their PSE lessons? We haven't asked them all, of course, but we'd wager that very few do. And that's probably, at least partly, because many teachers don't actually know anything about investment themselves. They never learned anything about it when they were young, they trust their own personal finances to the Wise, and they don't have any standard school textbooks on the subject.

Teaching material

Even if a school has a serious desire to teach personal finance and investment, it still faces a significant problem: lack of teaching materials. While the subject is not covered by the traditional curriculum, and while no exams are being set to measure our children's knowledge of personal finance, no educational textbooks will be written to teach the subject.

In some ways, though, that's probably a blessing. You can bet that if there were any kind of formal curriculum, and any recommended textbooks, they would be dull and boring. The books would be written by old fogeys from within the Wise establishment, and would probably push all sorts of academic nonsense. They'd be teaching portfolio theory and the theory of perfect markets, when the ability to understand companies and place long-term valuations on them is what really counts.

We'd see lessons concentrating on personal pension plans and how to choose the best unit trusts based on their past five years' performance figures (which, as we saw earlier, is nonsense, even though it is probably the most widely-used approach).

We'd see fixed formulae for how to split your savings between cash, gilts and shares. There's no such formula, of course, because it depends on your own individual circum-stances and your personal preferences, as much as anything (though at the Fool, we'd always advocate putting the bulk of your long-term savings into shares, stressing the 'long-term' part).

ProShare educational material

ProShare, a non-profit organization dedicated to furthering the cause of private investment (and who we shall meet in more detail in the next chapter, when we examine their National Investment Programme competitions), produces a package of teaching material that is aimed at helping teachers to teach personal finance within the bounds of the current school curriculum.

When thinking of how and where to teach personal finance and investing, none of the school subjects that we have considered so far fit the bill perfectly, but it is possible to utilize all of them to some degree to make the best of a bad situation. In fact ProShare have designed their teaching material to be applicable, in parts, to the current academic subjects of business studies, information technology, economics, mathematics, personal and social education, and citizenship, amongst others.

ProShare's educational material comes in the form of a publication for schools entitled *Your Money: Be Wise*. It's available free from the ProShare Web site (www.proshare.org) in the form of an Adobe PDF file. Despite the title ('Wise' being such a bad word in Foolish circles), it contains some useful stuff. It rather cleverly presents a number of sections and case studies that can be applied to all sorts of existing subjects. Do you reckon that any of its finance case studies might be applicable to English lessons? Or drama? No? Think again. If you're teaching English comprehension, why not throw in a modern subject that will be useful rather than some stodgy old prose from centuries ago? *Your Money* also includes teachers' notes describing exactly which part of the National Curriculum each exercise is aimed at, so there's no excuse for seeing it as irrelevant.

So, what subject matter does it cover? *Your Money* comes in three sections – 'Everyday budgeting', 'Business and shares', and 'Financial management for young people'. All very important to the needs of budding young Fools, but how Foolish is the stuff about shares?

Well, 'Business and shares' seems to focus more on business studies and less on the idea of personal investment (which is not surprising, given the need to stay within the curriculum), but it does a decent job of explaining what shares in public companies actually are, why people buy them, and what stock markets are all about. It doesn't really attempt to cover the accumulation of personal wealth through individual investment in any practical way, though, and so does not reveal the possibilities provided by a long-term approach to investing.

Also, to be honest, it tends to be a little dull, in the expected academic way. And there's one curious omission; when listing the reasons why share prices move, the long-term creation of new wealth (which is the only thing that moves share prices over the long term) is absent, and all we see is a list of short-term influences. Oh well.

This is a worthwhile piece of educational material, though, and most teachers who have responsibility for any of the academic subjects mentioned so far (and many of those who don't, too) should benefit from at least having a read of it. It's not sufficient on its own, and it won't make kids jump up and shout, 'I can be a millionaire; money is for ordinary people too.' But it gets a Foolish thumbs-up nonetheless.

What next?

We certainly want to see some decent financial education on offer in our schools as a central part of the curriculum, and although it may be a bit too optimistic to expect much change in the near future, we would urge you to do everything you can to help make it happen. Further down the line in Chapter Thirteen, we will be urging you, as a parent, to 'Nag your School'. Here, we're urging you to nag your MP, the Department of Education and anyone else who might have some bearing on the subject. It can be surprising just how effective popular movements can become in a short time and adding your voice to the campaign will help. We will, surely, see a revolution in the formal teaching of personal finance in schools one day.

But don't hold your breath.

In the meantime, what alternatives can the education service and individual schools offer?

Many schools do offer far more to their pupils than the formal curriculum and in fact, any that don't probably warrant some serious investigation. There are a number of initiatives outside the curriculum, ranging from the national level right down to individual schools, which definitely point children in the right direction, and in the next two chapters we will look at a couple of examples.

Put on your shorts, tie your hair in pigtails, pack up your pencil case, we're going back to school . . .

STOP PRESS

As we go to press, an exciting bit of news has just come in from the Foolish research department. We have always been convinced that teaching children and young people about finance and investment is a worthwhile thing to do. That's why we've written this book and if you're reading it, hopefully you agree with us. We believe that children of school age really can master the subject without too much trouble.

But how could we put it to the test? Remember those independent financial advisors (IFAs) we met in Chapter Seven? They can't just go around calling themselves IFAs without gaining some sort of accreditation first. No, they all have to sit an exam before they are allowed to go about their business. So, thought our research Fools, why don't we see what happens if we ask a small group of school students to sit part of the very same exam to see if they can grasp the concepts adequately?

We enlisted the help of Sunderland High School (who we'll hear a lot more about in Chapter Twelve) and they arranged for a group of volunteers to sit part of a real IFA exam after a short amount of tuition. They answered a set of sample questions selected

*from the Chartered Insurance Institute's Financial Planning
Certificate, which included questions about shares, ISAs, gilts,
insurance and so on. The group achieved an outstandingly
impressive average score of 93 per cent, with almost half of the
sample gaining full marks. Every single one of them scored 80 per
cent or more. Wow!*

*Conclusive proof that young people can handle basic financial
matters just as well as the professionals? We think so.*

Chapter Eleven: The ProShare Portfolio Challenge

Great contest follows, and much learned dust
Involves the combatants
William Cowper

The ProShare Portfolio Challenge is part of the ProShare National Investment Programme for Schools and Colleges, an initiative sponsored by ProShare that is aimed at increasing awareness of all matters related to personal finance. Sounds fair enough? We think so. We took a look at some of ProShare's educational material in the last chapter, and here we will examine their popular schools investment challenges, and the Portfolio Challenge in particular.

Before we look in any detail at the National Investment Programme, you'd probably like to know a little more about these noble-sounding people. ProShare is an organization that is active in three main areas, and we're probably best letting them tell it for themselves. So, take it away, ProShare. . .

'ProShare provides independent information and a variety of services designed to help and encourage private investors. It also provides information and assistance to investment clubs, which are an ideal way for people to learn about investing. ProShare lobbies Government and the relevant industry bodies to ensure that individual investment operates in a suitable tax and regulatory framework.

'ProShare aims to increase young people's ability to manage their finances and to understand the role of finance in the economy. It provides teaching materials and runs the National Investment Programme for Schools and Colleges. ProShare is also a leading participant in the debate on the need for greater emphasis on personal finance and business understanding in the National Curriculum.

'ProShare works with a number of leading advisors in the Employee Share Scheme field to promote the introduction and implementation of share schemes. As part of this aim, it provides comprehensive information, independent research and guidance to companies offering schemes or those interested in establishing them. In addition, ProShare lobbies strongly at senior level in Government and other organizations for a favourable tax and regulatory structure for employee share ownership. Through company focus groups, ProShare is currently working closely with the Inland Revenue to discuss and implement new employee share schemes that are intended to further encourage employee share ownership. ProShare also organizes a range of events throughout the year to provide companies with useful forums for learning more about the implementation, administration and communication of employee share schemes.'

ProShare is an independent non-profit organization, which was founded in 1992 with funding from the treasury, the London Stock Exchange, and 22 individual companies. Today, ProShare relies for support on a number of sponsors. And there are plenty of them – you can find a list on ProShare's Web site.

Of the areas that ProShare is working in, the young people's bit described above is obviously the one that we are mainly interested in here, but ProShare's encouragement of investment clubs is also something that you can put to good use in furthering your children's education. We will see why in the next chapter, but for now let's return to the National Investment Programme.

The National Investment Programme provides a set of teaching materials for use in schools, and we have already looked at some of that. The really fun part, though, is the annual challenge competitions.

The challenge competitions come in two forms. The first, the Portfolio Challenge, is the most relevant to potential Fools, so we'll look at that first and come back to the second, the Forecast Challenge, a little later.

The Portfolio Challenge

Imagine if teams of three or four pupils could each take a chunk of cash to the tune of £100,000 and invest it in the stock market. Also, imagine if those same teams were measured against each other and the ones whose investments performed the best won prizes. Well that's exactly how it works, except that the hundred grand isn't real. That would be too good to be true. It's an imaginary sum that the competitors are given to play with.

ProShare's initiative in setting up the challenge and running it every year is certainly worth applauding, but we think that there are a number of drawbacks to it, at least as far as educating children in the ways of the Fool. We will talk about these shortly, but in the meantime, while reading more of the Portfolio Challenge, see if you can pre-empt us and identify the things that we are going to be picky about. After all, if you've read this far, you should be pretty clued up about the way Fools handle their children's investments.

Any school or college in the UK can enter teams of three or four pupils in the Portfolio Challenge. Each school can enter as many teams as they want. The teams are pretty much free to invest in whatever share-based investments they choose, though there are a few restrictions. For full details of the rules, see the ProShare Web site, but here's a brief summary of how it works. . .

- All shares and other investments must be listed on ProShare's chosen ProShare 500 list of investments.
- All entries can be made online.
- Teams are responsible for monitoring their own portfolios.
- Success is dependent on portfolio performance.
- Each investment must consist of at least 5 per cent of the £100,000.
- Any uninvested cash will attract interest at an annual rate of 1.5 per cent.

The Portfolio Challenge is run each year, and is split into several stages. The dates for the 2000 to 2001 challenge are as follows:

- All portfolios need to be submitted by Friday 20 October 2000.
- A final valuation of all portfolios will be taken in early 2001.
- The top 100 teams from each region, based on financial performance, will then go on to the quarter finals.

During January and February 2001, the quarter-finalists must trade their portfolios and submit written reports for consideration by the judges, with the winning teams being chosen based on a combination of their reports and their trading performance. They will then go on to the semi-finals, with the finals taking place later in the year.

As well as the main competition prizes, extra prizes are awarded for the teams that achieve the best unit trust performance and the best investment trust performance.

The Forecast Challenge

The Forecast Challenge is aimed at younger children who perhaps don't have the time or the stamina for the Portfolio Challenge, and it is a lot simpler. It is run three times a year, and all the teams have to do is examine a list of ten companies (which is provided), and rank all ten according to their predicted growth rate. Oh, and an estimate from each team of the best performing share's actual percentage change (to two decimal places, no less) is also required, to be used in the event of a tie.

Each of the three runs of this challenge only lasts a few weeks, so the younger kids don't have to stick with it for very long.

A Fool's view

Now, before we attempt to analyze these two investment challenges in terms of the Foolish long-term ideal, we'd like to make one thing clear.

We are not disparaging ProShare's attempts to get financial education on to the curriculum at all. In fact, we heartily applaud their efforts, which we think put many of our schools today to shame. And the ProShare challenges are going to expose school children to the stock market and help to make them aware that investing is something that ordinary people, and young ones at that, can do successfully.

All that is far preferable to the ignorance and superstition that has for so long stood between ordinary people and their possible ownership of shares. But it is not a complete answer, not by a long way. Organized investment competitions are not a substitute for proper financial education (and we feel pretty sure ProShare would agree with us).

As far as the Foolish philosophy of investing for the long term in good companies goes, the ProShare challenges, if taken out of context and not used as just one part of a sound financial education, might prove a little dangerous in shaping our children's vision of investing. Here's why . . .

It's too short

The main problem, you see (and you will have probably

already guessed it), is that these challenges are very short term in nature. If they're going to fit into the academic year, they have to be really, and that is a hurdle that any form of practical investment exercise has to get over. But it can be done, as we will see in the next chapter.

The first phase of the ProShare Portfolio Challenge is held over a period of just two and a half months, and the teams are selected to go through to the next round on the basis of how well their portfolios have performed over this short period.

To be honest, this part of the challenge is a bit pointless. Over a period as short as that, nobody can hope to predict the direction of the stock market or of individual shares with any accuracy, and a winning portfolio will say absolutely nothing about the skill and judgement of the team that selected it. The performances of all of the teams' portfolios over those two and a half months, if plotted on a chart, would be very likely to result in the kind of bell-shaped graph that represents random variation (and it's off to Junior's GCSE maths textbook if you can't remember what that is). The reason for this is simple: the results will be random, pure and simple, and the teams that go through to the next round will have got through by luck, nothing else.

If we really could predict the stock market over such a short period, and if we were able to teach our children how to do it, then we would all have made it big and retired to the proverbial island in the sun, or at least Bournemouth, ages ago.

But this first stage of the competition isn't actually going to harm our kid's education, is it? Well, in fact, there's a danger that it might. The first problem is that there's a pretty good chance the participants will come away with the popular idea that the stock market is a short-term get-rich-quick lark. If such an important educational institution is running a short-term competition, and schools and colleges around the country are going along with it, then it must be a reasonable way to invest, right? Wrong!

The other thing to be wary of is the possibility that the kids whose teams make it through to the subsequent rounds might come away thinking that they actually have some skills in share selection, when all that has happened is that they have been pointed at by the finger of blind chance.

The subsequent rounds of the challenge are somewhat better, because the teams then have to submit a report that counts for a large portion of the marks awarded. But the performance of those portfolios is still a significant factor in the teams' success or failure. And even over a period as long as a whole year, stock market investing is still akin to gambling. There are very few people who can do well over so little time. There's a lot of luck, then, involved in winning the ProShare Portfolio Challenge, something the Fool's long-term approach seeks to eliminate.

'Now wait a minute!' you cry, 'What about Beat The Footsie? The Motley Fool has several mechanical strategies that involve buying shares according to various criteria and then holding them for just a year before rebalancing the portfolio.' Well, yes, the holding period we have chosen for those strategies (and they include the Relative Strength strategies too) is indeed one year. But that does not mean they are short-term strategies; far from it in fact. With our mechanical strategies, we expect to have bad years as well as good years (and the Beat The Footsie strategy, for example, has just had a pretty poor two-year period), and we have no idea whether one year is going to be good or bad. So, even though we advocate rebalancing those portfolios every year, they are not one-year strategies. In fact, we think you need to follow them for at least five years before you can have any real idea of how well you are doing, as is the case for all stock market investments.

Monopoly money

The other thing that is somewhat unreal about the Portfolio Challenge is the £100,000 slice of imaginary cash. It is unreal for two reasons. First, it isn't real (which is the most obvious way in which it is, erm, unreal). And that means that the teams investing it don't have the usual problem faced by investors, which is that it hurts to lose money. With an imaginary hundred grand to throw around, for which they won't be held accountable, kids can and will throw it at anything that looks like a short-term bubble in the hope of getting lucky. And if they lose the lot? Hey, who cares? It's not real money anyway.

How would the same children go about an investment challenge if they had, say, just a couple of thousand pounds of real money to invest? Would they gamble it recklessly and follow the latest hype in the hope of getting lucky, or would they be a little concerned about how much they could lose if it went wrong? All this may sound trite (of course it's only imaginary money! Where would they get the real stuff from?), but we took the trouble to talk to some sixth formers (admittedly, quite smart ones, who we will meet in the next chapter), and the answer is quite clear. Playing with imaginary money is only ever going to be seen as a game, and nobody is likely to worry about losing the stuff. But investing real money is a different thing altogether, and the responsibility that goes with it requires an entirely different approach. If you're investing imaginary money over a very short time period in an attempt to win a competition, the sensible thing to do is to punt it on the latest trend, the most high-risk investment you can find. If it comes off, hey, you've won! But if it doesn't, you haven't lost anything. That's totally unlike investing in the real world.

The second unreality is the amount itself. Doesn't it tend to reinforce the idea that the stock market is only for the wealthy? If the teams have £100,000 to invest in the competition, isn't that going to make them feel that it isn't worth investing a sum as lowly as £25 a month? Well, after asking more questions, we discovered that children do indeed come away from competitions like this thinking that the stock market is only for people with big money to invest.

But we have seen the princely sums that can be accumulated by investing as little as £25 a month over a long period. Do we want our children to be scared away from that and leave school thinking that the stock market is only for those who are already stinking rich? Or do we want them to understand that successful stock market investing is for them too, and they really don't have to accumulate a huge pile first? We know what our answer is. What's yours?

League table

On to that Forecast Challenge for younger pupils. What they have to do is rank ten given companies according to how they guess their share prices will perform over the next couple of months. Now that really is pointless, and will teach the children absolutely nothing at all about the stock market or about personal finance. However well the children can analyze and understand the ten companies they are presented with, this will have little or no correlation to their share price movements over such a short period. Great companies frequently fall over the short term, and long-term losers often do well for limited periods. This kind of competition is surely only going to confuse the kids.

What next?

Having told you how much we admire ProShare's noble aims, and then gone on to poke a few holes in their Portfolio Challenge, are there any things that we think would improve competitions of this type?

Well, yes, there are, though the practicalities of administering such things might get in the way somewhat. First, that first round really should contain something more than just the 'first past the post' portfolio competition. While it would be impractical to handle written reports from every single team taking part, some sort of portfolio analysis might be possible. How about looking at the amount of diversification that the teams have built into their portfolios, for example? In real life, many investors offset the risk inherent in each of their individual investments by spreading their money across different industries and different market sectors (though Foolish investors will always be careful never to diversify into poor quality companies just for the sake of it). Could the teams' strategies be assessed this way? It would, at least, eliminate all those who just jumped on the 1999 'dot com' bandwagon and saw all sorts of vaguely Internet-related companies soar in value. It's not the answer, but it's just a thought.

It would also be great to see the schools involved treating this as a single part of a more general education – we'd love to see them putting the emphasis on long-term investment and pointing out the inevitable shortfalls of a short-term competition.

And that £100,000? How about throwing this away and giving the teams £10,000, or maybe even just £5,000 to invest? That might make them feel that you don't have to be extremely wealthy to invest in the stock market, and that it really is open to mere mortals with more realistic sums of money. Perhaps they'll think, 'Hmm, that's the kind of money that my parents invest, and that I could easily accumulate if I'm careful, so maybe we should treat this like a real investment.'

The whole approach of involving children in realistic practical exercises as part of their education is essential, we think. After all, how much chemistry would kids learn if they never attempted to blow up the lab (sorry, carried out controlled experiments) themselves?

But is there a better, longer term, and more realistic way to go about it? You bet there is, and we'll look at the achievements of one successful school in the next chapter.

Chapter Twelve: Sunderland High School

'Tis education forms the common mind,
Just as the twig is bent, the tree's inclined.
Alexander Pope

We've heard how rational Foolish investors go about profitable long-term investing, and we've heard the occasional quote from one or two of them, too. We have, of course, also heard the way the Wise doyens of the financial services industry try to tell it. We are going to start this chapter with a few more quotes, and here are some that we think are particularly good. Try to guess where we might have got them from as we go along. . .

'When buying shares we chose mostly blue chips.'

That's a good one, don't you think? Of all the investing styles that you could go for when you start out on the road to choosing your own companies, going for blue chip companies is probably the safest one to start with (and remember, 'blue chip' is just the term used to describe big solid companies, the pillars of the economy). Choosing companies for yourself gives you real control over your own investments and provides the incentive needed to actually analyze some companies and get to know them well (and there's no substitute for investing real money when it comes to providing an incentive for doing it properly). Blue chips are, after all, the companies that make up the bulk of a FTSE 100 index tracker. So, was this one of the

Motley Fool's founders, talking about their early days? Nope!

'Anything can happen to change share prices in the short term.'

Too right it can, and far too many investors get overexcited by the short-term ups and downs of their share prices. Over the short term, all sorts of emotional factors affect a share price. Usually, it is only over the long term that a company's fundamental strengths show through. So the Dow Jones falls 3 per cent in one day, and the FTSE follows the next day; does that change the fundamental value of companies that you hold? No, of course not; but every day we see investors buying and selling frantically on the back of short-term market indicators, ignoring the long-term strength of their investments.

Understanding and accepting the fact that share prices fluctuate a lot in the short term, and refusing to be affected by it, is a key part of long-term investing success. So, where did we get this quote? From a well-known fundamentalist giving a lesson on the perils of following short-term prices? Nah!

'It's all about having a long term vision, really.'

This is one of our favourites, and it sums up the entire Foolish investment strategy in one simple statement. Accepting the need for a long-term strategy is an essential part of investing success, we think. But the best long-term investors aren't just people who accept that need; they are people who actually possess the vision too.

It's not too hard a vision to get used to either; just think back ten or twenty years and remember how much less material wealth people used to have (OK, schoolchildren reading this will have a little trouble doing that, but you must have heard stories from your parents about how much harder it was for them, and how much less they had in the way of luxuries when they were young). Now project that into the future, because there is no real evidence that the world's overall economic expansion is going to come to a halt any time soon, and think what your children and your grandchildren will be able to achieve.

So we all need to get our heads around the long-term vision:

the prospect of greater and greater wealth for coming generations. It's not that hard really, is it?

But who was the author of this quote? Warren Buffett, the world's greatest long-tem investor, or one of his associates? No, not him!

The school investment club

Those three quotes, along with plenty more sensible words on investing (some of which we will hear shortly), came from a half a dozen sixth formers (and ex-sixth formers) at Sunderland High School, with whom your Foolish author had the privilege of spending a day, discussing their school investment club.

Yes, a school investment club; investing real money; parents' money included. And it was a long-term project too, with the portfolio handed on from year to year, from one management team to the next. Now how's that for concentrating young minds on the reality of investing? Don't you think it beats the idea of a short-term fantasy investment competition with hundreds of thousands of fantasy pounds to invest?

It was all the brainchild of Peter Hogan, deputy head of Sunderland High School, who started up the school investment club, known as the Fiderium Trust, a few years ago. Peter, who teaches business studies in addition to his deputy head duties, realized how little education in personal finance and investment the school curriculum actually provided, and wanted to do something practical about it. Understanding the limitations of short-term competitions and investing using fantasy money, he quickly came to the conclusion that useful practical education best comes from real investing using real money.

Running the club

The Fiderium Trust is run as a real investment club, with the club members being drawn mainly from the ranks of the school's parents and teachers. The practicalities of running the club, from appointing a chairman, treasurer, and secretary, to all the research and the investment decisions, are handled by four pupils appointed each year for a one-year period.

The selection of the four 'managers' is done in as realistic a manner as possible; candidates have to apply for the positions and sit interviews, just as they would for a real job. It can't just be treated as a game; you've got to be serious to get a position with the Fiderium Trust. Education, after all, is supposed to prepare young people for real life, so the closer to real life it is, the better. And it is real money after all.

It is the responsibility of each year's club managers to provide regular reports to the club members, to share research, to manage the practicalities of running the bank accounts and stockbrokers' accounts, and to handle the mechanics of actually making share purchases. Everything, in fact, just as they would in a real investment club; because that's exactly what it is.

The important long-term continuity of the endeavour is maintained too. It would be easy to liquidate the club's assets each year and hand over cash for the next four managers to play with; they could start again with a clean slate and nobody's previous successes and failures to contend with. (And that, by the way, is how some 'Wise' publications handle their own model portfolios: if they're not doing too well, they change the manager and start again from scratch.) But that wouldn't be like real life, would it? No, instead, each year's managers take over the club exactly as the previous bunch left it; the existing portfolio, the same accounts and records, the lot.

And the benefits show through. James Donald had this to say: 'We got a lot of support from the outgoing people from last year. They did very well and helped us a lot.' The outgoing managers have a vested interest in helping the newcomers to take over successfully – it is, after all, their baby and they want it taken care of.

Investment clubs

Investment clubs provide a great springboard for any novice investor. Many potential investors are deterred by the amount of work that they think they'll have to do and lack the confidence to go it alone. But being part of a club allows you to spread the work and, more importantly, provides support for your investment decisions. Just think: if you've got, say, a dozen members in your investment club, you have twelve times as much grey matter to bring to bear on your analysis and decisions. And twelve ways to spread the responsibility for bad decisions!

The other big advantage, of course, is that an investment club is all about the pooling of money. And that means that individuals can get started in investment with a relatively small bankroll. Just £25 per member per month, say, soon adds up to a reasonably sized investment chunk.

If you want to find out more about investment clubs, then we'd suggest that *The Motley Fool's Guide to Investment Clubs*, by Mark Goodson, is what you want. Available directly from Fool Books on the Motley Fool Web site, at ***www.fool.co.uk***, it's packed with information and is based on Mark's extensive real-life experience of running a number of investment clubs.

Another essential is ProShare's guide to investment clubs, details of which can be found on the ProShare Web site, at ***www.proshare.org***. Amongst other things, it covers the details of the legal requirements that you need to take care of, because investment clubs are legal entities (though there is not actually very much that you really need to do). It also contains examples of all of the necessary documentation, which you can photocopy for use by your own club.

And finally, we think investment clubs are such a great way to start investing Foolishly that we have started the Motley Fool Staff Investment Club. All members are Motley Fool staff (as you might have guessed), we invest real money (£25 each per month), and our club's proceedings, decisions, and investment performance are covered on our own discussion board on the site. If you are interested in running a club, our experiences will hopefully be of some help to you.

Who are they?

Most of the information so far about the Sunderland High School club came from Peter himself, as he is becoming quite well-known at the Motley Fool. But we needed to find out just how well the school investment club idea was working as an educational exercise, and there was only one way to do that – talk to the kids themselves. (Apologies for the use of the term 'kids' is called for here. Whatever they were, the people running this club weren't kids; but there's no short snappy word to describe seventeen and eighteen-year olds who are at school. And 'young adults' sounds so patronising.)

So off trekked the author one sunny spring day, all the way across the Pennines to the Northeast to meet up with these aspiring young Rothschilds and Buffetts and see just what they thought about it all. Two of the last year's managers (that's the 1998-1999 year), Guy McNulty and James Arrowsmith, who had since gone off to university, were tracked down; and a good bit of time was spent chatting to the current year's managers too (1999-2000) – Natalie Forster, James Donald, Zoe Marshall and Emily Thomas. Many thanks are due to all six, without whom this section of the book just wouldn't have existed. And these six, of course, are responsible for the quotes that illuminate this chapter.

What did they think?

The first thing that was clear about these six was that they were in deadly earnest about what they were doing. This was no game; it was a serious challenge and they wanted to do well. They had, after all, gone through a demanding selection process in the first place, and they weren't going to let the opportunity go to waste. And it was real money too, but what difference did that make? Quite a bit, as it happens.

Sunderland High School students also take part in the ProShare National Investment Programme and compete in the Portfolio Challenge (which we looked at in the last chapter).

Some of our investment club managers had some first-hand experience of that, so how did the club compare with it in terms of educational value? Here's what several of them said. . .

'With a fantasy share trading game, who cares? It's not real money. From an educational point of view it was a lot better for us because the investment club actually showed our responsibility. And even if we lost money, we'd learn from our decisions.' – Guy McNulty

'It wouldn't have been the same running it as a fantasy portfolio, it's the fact that it's real money that makes all the difference, because it puts real responsibilities on your shoulders. If it's fantasy money, you just wouldn't make your decisions the same way at all.' – Natalie Forster

'The virtual portfolio competition may be a good way of getting some idea of the mechanics, but so far as gaining confidence goes, you're going to be far more sure of yourself in the end if you've actually been investing real money.' – James Arrowsmith

It's clear that these people didn't treat short-term investment competitions as serious exercises in investment or share selection, seeing them more as games that you win by luck. They did, however, gain some benefit from them by learning a little about the mechanics of share buying. But how did that compare with actually buying and selling real shares, with real money, using a real stockbroker? It didn't come close.

Their experience with the Fiderium Trust taught them a good few valuable lessons about the world of investment and, in particular, helped them to see through the smoke and mirrors that surround the world of professional investing. It's only mysterious because 'it's dressed up in all this wonderful financial language, isn't it?' said Guy, and how right he was.

And how about the Wise telling us that ordinary people

can't handle their own investments? Here's what Zoe had to say about that. . .

> *'We just came in blind. We'd had a year of business studies and we came in and took over, and now we can say to people "look what we've done, it really is quite easy." At the beginning you think, "Oh, I can't do this," but then you start to realize it's not that hard; it's not what people think it is.'*

Well said, Zoe.

But does all this bring home the need for, and the lack of, personal finance education in the UK? You bet it does. Here's what Emily thought. . .

> *'We all need to understand money, and they teach you absolutely nothing. They're much more conscientious about money matters over in the USA though. I was watching a programme on telly that showed young children being taught in schools, and they had five jars with different money in. They had, for example, jars for immediate money, tax money, and all that sort of thing.'*

It sounds like American children are taught more about the importance of managing money from an early age. It's no wonder, then, that they lead the world in economic development, is it?

What else did they learn?

The Fiderium Trust taught far more than just investment. It taught, amongst other things, the value of teamwork and co-operation, the need for and the power of communication, the critical need to establish good customer relations (all those parents were breathing down their necks and needed to be satisfied that they weren't buying a pig in a poke), and the need for delegation and the power that division of labour brings to joint endeavours.

Negotiation skills also came to the fore, as the club members approached various stockbrokers and bank managers to see what help they could give. And before anyone cries, 'But you'd have more chance of getting blood out of a stone than getting help from a bank manager,' the experience was apparently very positive and they got plenty of practical support.

And that's the kind of thing that Peter was after, really, when he started the whole thing up. Here's what he had to say. . .

'There's a range of things, that's always been my objective. You've got to work as a group, work together, approach strangers and ask them for money. . .'

Powerful stuff, as long as they don't take the idea of approaching strangers and asking them for money too far!

The Fiderium Trust was also a great way of getting individuals to learn new skills in areas in which they were relatively weak. It would have been easy for everyone to jump into the roles that best suited their individual skills, but that's not the way they went about it. No, in many cases they directed themselves to their weaker areas, because that way they learned more and expanded their horizons further.

Peter again. . .

'I like the way they thoughtfully got Tanya to do all the word processing when she was the one with the least IT experience. They empowered her.'

We didn't meet Tanya, unfortunately, but it is clear that she used her time with the Fiderium Trust as an opportunity to strengthen her skills in an area in which she was unfamiliar.

And one final lesson that they all learned; one that everyone should keep close to their hearts. . .

'We made mistakes, but that's the thing. You are going to make mistakes in the stock market.'

In fact, you're going to make mistakes in life: period. And anyone who sets out unprepared for them, expecting never to do anything wrong, is asking for trouble.

All told then, a pretty well-rounded educational exercise, it seems.

What did their parents think?

Without exception, the parents were wholly supportive of their sons' and daughters' involvement in the Fiderium Trust, and a number of them were happy to hand over some of their cash to be used for investment purposes. Whether they treated it as a serious investment proposal, or simply as support for their children's education, is an interesting question. But it doesn't really matter so much; it's the willingness to offer support that counts.

They certainly seemed to be taking it seriously, though, and a number of them were pretty forthright when it came to tightening the screws and putting the club managers though their paces. But parents need to watch out, and should never underestimate the knowledge and insight that their offspring may possess. One or two of the club managers saw through it – they noticed the ritual nature of some of the questions and wondered how much their parents really understood, and they certainly observed one or two winks passing betwixt Mum and Dad. But we're not going to name names here.

And even if at the start, the parents might not have been convinced by the potential success that the fruits of their loins might achieve, they were hopefully pleasantly surprised at the end of it. In fact, at the outset. . .

> 'When we told them we were going to be doing stocks and shares, they'd say, "Oh yeah, Mickey Mouse money," but it's real money and if anything went wrong, it was our fault.' – Zoe

But by the end. . .

*'They saw it wasn't like pupils just doing something to be sold
to parents; they saw it was quite professionally done.'* – Guy

Fame and the future

The Fiderium Trust gained its fair share of fame during its
lifetime, and a number of newspapers and magazines beat a trail
to the school doors to report on this strange phenomenon –
sixth formers taking on the complicated and difficult task of
handling investment, and actually doing a pretty good job of it.

In fact, even the venerable and crusty Wall Street Journal
wanted to know about them.

But you know what? There wasn't a bighead amongst them,
and they all treated their experiences and their achievements
with a humility that many in the financial services industry
would do well to emulate.

The Fool's visit to Sunderland High School coincided with
a little bit of sadness, as this was the last year (as far as anyone
could tell at the time) that the Fiderium Trust would be run,
and the club was in the process of winding down and
liquidating its assets.

The guiding hand of the club, deputy head Peter Hogan,
was moving on, you see. He was moving to another school and
at the time of writing nobody had stepped in with an offer to
oversee the club next year. The good Mr H, however, is
working on a whole host of new ideas for practical education
in investment, and the students at his new school, Llandovery
College in Camarthenshire, clearly have some exciting times
ahead of them.

Your school can do it too

*As the experience of Sunderland High School shows, it really isn't
hard to set up a school investment club and to get some seriously*

useful practical education in place. You will probably have little difficulty in attracting interest too, as the pupils and parents in Sunderland showed.

All a school really needs is an experienced and willing teacher to organize things and keep an eye on everything. The teacher in charge needn't necessarily be teaching business studies or any other relevant discipline; he or she just needs some experience in the mechanics of investing in the stock market.

Peter Hogan, who started the whole Sunderland thing, is currently hatching new plans and intends to develop the idea of investing in schools further. He is also available to offer help to other schools who might be interested.

From the Autumn 2000 academic year onwards, Peter can be contacted at his new school, Llandovery College, in Camarthenshire. He can be reached by e-mail at llan.col@virgin.net
Alternatively, by traditional post, he can be reached at. . .
Llandovery College
Llandovery
Camarthenshire
SA20 0EE
If you do contact Peter for more information, don't forget to say 'Hi' from the Fool.

And the club managers at the school? It's quite clear that their experience of investing in the stock market has opened their eyes to how easy it is for them to go about investing for themselves, and how much nonsense the professionals spout in order to maintain their aura of mystery and to keep the rich pickings from their fat commissions. But will they manage their own investments once they are out in the big wide world and earning their crusts for themselves? We asked them, and we can sum up their response with a pretty representative answer. . .

> *'Now [after this experience] I'd seriously consider investing in the stock market. And I'd be keen to make the decisions as to what shares to buy myself.'*

And their performance? When the club started out, everyone involved would have been happy if they'd broken even and not lost any of their parents' money. In fact, we asked them what, if they look back in ten years' time, they will most remember about their year with the school investment club. And the answer? It was a pretty unanimous. . .

> 'We didn't lose money.'

That's a pretty good way to start out on your personal investment career, don't you think? Too many investors (or perhaps we should say 'gamblers') get stars in their eyes when they start thinking of the untold riches that lie ahead, if only they can jump on to the latest fad and jump off again at just the right time, and a lot of that attitude probably stems from their late entry into the world of investment. 'This long-term stuff is all very well,' they might say, 'but it's too late for me now. I need a quick profit.' Warren Buffett, who started young, has never done it that way and his results speak for themselves. Our children, too, need have no fears of getting in too late provided we teach them early enough. And it looks like the Fiderium Trust has taught that lesson rather well.

So not losing money was the bottom line. But as it happens, the Fiderium Trust beat the FTSE, and in doing so, these young, inexperienced, untrained, but clearly very Foolish investors beat at least 93 per cent of the professionals who manage the UK's unit trusts and investment trusts.

And that, we think, is something to be proud of. We'll leave the last words of this chapter to Fiderium Trust co-manager Natalie. . .

> 'We've actually done pretty well, and we've outdone the Footsie. We've certainly done better than we expected. An important point is that that we're just sixth formers and we've done all right. There are proper investment companies out there that get paid loads of money and do so badly.'

Chapter Thirteen: What can parents do?

Children aren't happy with nothing to ignore,
And that's what parents were created for.
Ogden Nash

Invest for your kids, that's the thing to do, and hand the whole lot over when they reach the age of 18. That much we've already worked out. But if they've learned nothing during their formative years about the value of long-term investing and the need to provide life-long security for themselves, then there's a good chance that the ingrates will immediately rush out and blow a huge chunk of that nest egg on parties, holidays, and loads of flash things that they really don't need.

Of course they need to have fun when they're 18, but when you've worked so hard to stash away that £25 a month (or however much you could afford) for all those years, do you want your kids to blow it all? Unlikely, we'd guess. And the answer is education.

In the last chapter, we saw what can be achieved at schools if the willingness and enthusiasm are there, but it is rare for anything approaching that level of endeavour to be achieved in practice. So it's down to parents, in the end, to instil into children that all-important awareness of the need for sound financial management and a life-long approach to investment. We have also seen, though, that children learn far, far better when it's something that they want to learn, something that they can develop a passion for, than when something is being foisted upon them, albeit by well-meaning adults.

Try to guess which of the following parents is more likely to end up with children educated Foolishly; one who goes for. . .

'*No Johnny*, you can't go out tonight. You know Thursday is compound interest day. Now get your books out and stop looking so miserable!'

Or one who approaches it more like this. . .

'*Hey, Jane, can you spare an hour? Your Dad and I are thinking about our next stock market investment; do you fancy helping us with our decision?*'

By the time they reach adulthood, Jane is going to be much better prepared for handling her own finances than Johnny, isn't she? Unfortunately, a good few parents today still seem to think that you really can put old heads on young shoulders and that to educate, all you need to do is lecture. Such parents probably do deserve to be ignored, and we can sympathize with Ogden Nash on that one.

Learning through experience

Learning comes through wanting to learn, and the desire to learn comes from day-to-day experience. So getting children directly involved in personal finance from an early age can pay handsome dividends later. In the early years, when sizeable sums are still a few years in the future, simply getting your kids to save money is a great way to start.

When it come to finding an apt way to express something, the Motley Fool's resident doting dad Nigel Roberts (OK, we've got a few doting dads at the Fool, but Nigel does seem to dote a bit more publicly than most) often seems to be the one to come up with the goods. Let's hear a few words from him on the subject of teaching your children to save. . .

I was recently reading some messages at the US Fool, in the Family Fool message board (yes, those Americans have a board for everything) when I came across the following quote: "Be a good role model. Children are more likely to be good savers if they see that their parents save regularly and find saving money to be worthwhile" It really does sound simple, doesn't it? But I do think that teaching our children to save and save regularly is one of the most important things we do for them. Certainly the best way to teach them is through setting a good example – my wife and I both learned the importance of saving from our parents, and we intend to pass that lesson on to our daughter.'

Hear, hear!

Get them saving early

What we'd suggest, then, is that as soon as a child is old enough to start receiving regular pocket money, he or she is old enough to start saving. But that saving has to be done in a way that the child understands. Too young to understand what a bank is? Then encourage the use of a piggy bank, and help to show just how much those spare pennies saved each week can add up when it comes to holidays, Christmas and birthdays.

As soon as a child is old enough to understand the idea of a bank, opening a savings account should become top priority, and the little one should be involved at every stage. Take them along every time money is paid in (and taken out, even), and encourage them to save any cash presents that they get for birthdays. Well, actually, we're not total scrooges here, so by all means let them spend a bit as well, as long as they understand the importance of saving some of it.

Make sure they understand the concept of interest too, again when they're old enough, and help them to learn about the way money, when used sensibly, generates more of itself. These are probably the most important concepts to get across to children – that amounts of money don't stay fixed; that wealth can be used to create more wealth; and that small amounts of money can quite easily be turned into large amounts of money.

And don't forget to teach by example too, so make a point of letting your kids know that you are saving money yourself, and that you have always done so since you were little (if you have been, that is!).

Of course, all this 'educational' saving can be separate from the regular savings and investments that you yourself make on behalf of your children. And that's fine early on, because the real purpose behind getting children to save small amounts of pocket money for themselves is education. A child who understands the value of saving pocket money is far more likely to grow into an adult who saves and invests money sensibly than one who never saves a penny.

But when they've grown up a bit, why not also get them involved in the savings and investments that you are making on their behalf? That money they are building up in shares, held in a bare trust, should be something to capture their imagination. And the fact that they have shares of their own (albeit ones they can't touch until they're 18) should provide a real incentive towards understanding what companies are and why you would want to own shares in them. It's going to be much easier teaching them this way than trying to get them interested in learning about the stock market with nothing practical to relate it to.

Don't keep them in the dark

Some people advocate keeping children in the dark regarding the pile that you are slowly building up for them, for a number of reasons. Maybe you think that children shouldn't be bothered with money at too young an age; perhaps you're worried that they will grow up less than humble if they realize that there's a pot of riches waiting for them, or you may even be concerned that they'll get anxious in times when stock markets are a bit rocky and the short-term value of their investments is falling.

Some of those are valid concerns, but whatever your reasons for being hesitant to introduce your children to the ins and outs of their own investments, we firmly believe that the benefits will far outweigh any fears that you might have.

Fool writer Yvonne Ravenhall summed it up nicely in a discussion board post not so long ago, when she wrote. . .

> *'I'm surprised that many folks seem to think that their offspring are best kept in the dark about the nest egg which is planned for them. Please, don't let the next generation grow up as ignorant of personal finance as most of us did. That's condemning them to repeat our disasters as they learn the hard way. As soon as the kids have mastered multiplication (which is all you need to work out compound growth), it's time to start involving them in the exercise. By all means keep your hand on the reins (and the money). But tell them why you chose the investments you did; what the performance has been; how to track the instruments in the newspapers or online.'*

Many parents carry their fear a little further and become afraid to hand the money over when their children reach 18 (which is a legal requirement for bare trusts), in case they blow the lot and put paid to all those long years of careful investment. To prevent that happening, some go as far as investigating different kinds of trusts; ones in which you can keep the proceeds tied up until the beneficiaries reach the age of 21, or 35, 96 or whatever. But if you go along that path, as we explained in Chapter Nine, you'll be starting to tread on more complex legal ground, and you'll need the services of lawyers. Those don't come cheap, and you have to start asking yourself if you really want to be lining your lawyers' pockets instead of your kids'.

Judging by the messages posted on the Fool's Investing For Children discussion board, most people believe that education really is the way to avoid such problems, and at the Fool, we heartily concur with this sentiment. The earlier your children are exposed to their own investments, the keener they will be to understand what they are all about and how this investment business works, and the less likely they'll be to spend their windfall when they reach 18.

The most common fear we hear is the old 'I know what I was like at 18; what if they turn out to be the same?' Think back to your own 18th birthday for a moment, and ponder what you would have done if you'd been handed a stash of valuable share certificates. If you think you'd have sold them and spent the money on having a good time, don't despair. Instead, think back a bit further, to your upbringing and education. Were you taught about the importance of investment from an early age? Were you an avid saver as a child? Or did you reach the age of 18 in splendid ignorance of the ways of the stock market and the wonders of compound returns? If the latter sounds more like you, maybe the secret is to make sure that your own kids aren't like you when they reach 18, and that they reach adulthood with a much better grounding than you did.

But what if, after all your efforts, the irresponsible wretches do indeed cash in those investments and spend the lot? Well, if you've done your best to teach them from an early age and they haven't got it by 18, is a couple more years going to make much difference? It's their lives and their money after all; and they've got to make their own decisions some day.

It's your choice though.

Family finance

A logical next step, after exposing your children to the excitement of their own investments, is to get them involved in family investments. Do you have your own regular savings? How did you choose where to put them? Do you invest in the stock market yourself? How do you make your individual investment decisions?

All these things should provide valuable educational experience for your children, so why not get them involved? There's no need to disclose how much money you've got, or the size of your investment chunks, but just think how important your kids will feel if they are trusted to take part in your analysis and decisions. And if they are anything like the Sunderland High School sixth formers we met in the last chapter, maybe you should pay attention to what they have to say, too – education does work both ways, after all.

Nag your school

How well does your children's school teach personal finance and investing? If the school is in any way typical, the chances are that it does a pretty poor job of it. Having read thus far, how do you feel about that now? Do you think that your kids are being short-changed when it comes to such an important practical subject?

You do?!

Well tell that to the school! Write to the head teacher asking why such scant attention is being paid to something so important, and ask what plans they have for the future.

And don't forget those parents' evenings. They're designed for you to say what you think, not just for teachers to tell you how your children are doing, and there's no reason why you should constrain your discussion to the children themselves. So question the school. Point out how important you think it is to be able to manage money, and how much you'd like to see your children learning something about it.

You may well find that the responses you get are based more on ignorance than anything. But now you have plenty of material to support your views. And if the school has any doubts about the relevance of financial education to subjects covered by the National Curriculum, you could always give them a copy of this book and point them in the direction of ProShare's *Your Money: Be Wise*, which we described in Chapter Ten.

If you were impressed by the achievements of Sunderland High School and would like to see a similar scheme set up in your own children's school, you might like to tell them all about it. Suggest they set up something similar, and tell them they can find out more by contacting the man behind Sunderland High School's success (whose contact details can be found in Chapter Twelve).

Introduce them to the Fool

The Motley Fool Web site welcomes young people, and provides a forum for thousands of private investors to share their experiences. It runs two real money portfolios, based on different share selection criteria, with regular reports published on the site for all to see. The main aim of these two portfolios is to provide education (though we really won't mind if they turn out to be profitable too!)

The Fool also carries news, company information, company profiles, share prices, and hundreds of separate discussion boards dedicated to discussing individual companies.

To register with the Motley Fool, which allows you to post messages, create portfolios, and customize the site to your preferences, you need to certify that you are at least 18 years of age. So if you want your children to benefit, you will need to register in your own name, and exercise parental control and guidance over any activities that you carry out with your kids.

You don't need to register to read the site; you just won't be able to post messages and customize anything if you don't.

And that brings us nicely to the greatest resource that private investors (parents or children) have at their disposal. We're talking about the most important technological development to have hit the world in decades – a great step forward in the promotion of free speech and the breaking down of jealously guarded barriers to information.

Yes, we're talking about the Internet, and no book on investment would be complete without a few words about it.

Are you ready? Then turn the page!

Chapter Fourteen: The Internet

It's a load of over-hyped rubbish, the Internet. It might be fun for geeks, but normal people will never be able to find their way through the rubbish that's on it.
Alan Oscroft, sometime in early 1995.

We all get things wrong, sometimes quite spectacularly. But look back just four or five years: how many people would have predicted the rapid spread and the unstoppable power of the Internet? The Internet was one of the pivotal technological developments of the 20th century, and is right up there alongside aviation, computers, and Chicken McNuggets.

What inroads has the Internet made in Britain? Back in 1994, there were an estimated 1 million people using the Internet in the UK. By the end of 1999, that figure stood at approximately 10 million: a tenfold increase in just five years. And the future? It's difficult to predict, of course, but there appears to be a consensus estimate of around 30 million users by 2005, which accounts for around half the current UK population, but doesn't account for the almost universal use of the wireless Internet that is expected by then.

Most of those new users will be young people, and Internet usage will be close to saturation amongst that group if the estimates turn out to be accurate. From then onwards, the number of users will grow more slowly, and will most likely follow the birth rate closely for the next decade or two.

But that is only half the story, because future growth in the number of new users will account for a relatively small proportion of the total growth in Internet usage. 'What's he talking about?' you may ask. 'Who's going to make up the rest of the growth? Pixies?' No, the extra growth will come from existing users who will use the Internet for more and more things.

A week in the life

What do I use the Internet for? And what would constitute a typical week's Web surfing for me?

Here are a few of the things I used it for in the course of a week recently. . .

*Human psychology is something that fascinates me, particularly as it relates to investment and our innate tendency towards emotion rather than logic. I am also fascinated by evolution. So I recently wrote a piece for the Fool site (**www.fool.co.uk**) on the subject of investor psychology, and the evolutionary aspects of our ability to handle numbers and probabilities. The next day I read some feedback that it generated on the Fool discussion boards. One Fool recommended a book that, while rather academic, was considered by many to be a milestone in the study of evolutionary psychology. I checked out the Amazon.com sites, both the US site (**www.amazon.com**) and the UK site (**www.amazon.co.uk**), and found 13 reader reviews in total, most of which were very favourable. That was enough, and I ordered a copy (Amazon's one-click ordering makes it oh-so-easy). It arrived the next day.*

The same week, I was at a friend's house and he was concerned that his computer was very slow. I checked, and found it didn't really have enough memory. 'You need some more memory', I said. 'Where do I get that from?' he asked. 'Why, the Internet is your best bet', I answered brightly. It took about half an hour to check out a bunch of computer suppliers and find the best price for the memory *that was needed, and it was ordered (**www.novatech.co.uk**). Two days later, it arrived.*

*Then another friend, Graham, popped round. 'Here's an Internet thingy I've found, about fishing in Scotland. How does it work? Can you look it up?' he asked, showing me an Internet address that he'd found in a magazine. Thirty seconds later, there it was (**www.fishing-scotland.co.uk/**). Graham had never looked at the Internet before, so I did a bit of searching too (**www.google.com**) and found a whole load of other relevant sites. And was he impressed? Judging by the look on his face, you'd have thought I'd just turned water into wine.*

I also checked on my own investment portfolio, kept an eye open for news about the companies I'm interested in, swapped a few messages on the Fool discussion boards, and sent and received lots of e-mail.

Oh, and I did a week of Fool work too, of course, but that's my job.

People will buy books, CDs and videos (oh, they already do). Supermarkets, computer suppliers, booking agencies, airlines, hotels: all sorts of retail businesses are starting to offer online sales. The reason is simple. It's cheaper. There's no need to maintain high street shops, which are frequently in the most expensive parts of town. Distribution networks can be built around costs and efficiency too. And there is frequently no middleman to pay at all: no frills airline easyJet, for example, only sells direct; you can't make an easyJet booking through a travel agent.

The future of traditional shops has been made clear, and many of them will not be around in their current form in a decade or so because they just can't compete with such a powerful new medium.

The Internet is making great inroads in education too. Although a very large number of older people do not use the Internet at all, with many never having even seen it, approximately 95 per cent of schoolchildren have access to the Internet at school.

But nothing mentioned so far has anything to do with investing, so what's the point? Simple. If you don't get online, you'll get left behind.

The Internet for investors

Why is it only in recent years that the facades of the old Wise financial institutions have started to crack, and ordinary people have started to see how easy it is for them to take responsibility for their own financial wellbeing? It's not that people didn't care, or weren't intelligent enough to understand. No, of course it wasn't. It's just that people didn't know. Information is the key, and the control of information was the cornerstone of the financial institutions' power. If ordinary people couldn't gain access to the same information that the professionals had at their fingertips, then the professionals could control it and charge for it. And charge handsomely at that.

The Internet has changed all that, and for the first time in history, ordinary everyday people have an open, uncontrolled, and uncensored forum for the interchange of information and opinion. Want to research a particular company as a possible investment? What's better then, to pay through the nose for a professional analyst's report (and remember, opinions amongst the professionals can be just as diverse and contradictory as the opinions of amateurs), or to get news and performance data about the company from Internet Web sites and then use Internet discussion boards to share your findings with other private investors and to examine the opinions of others?

The facilities that are now available for private investors via the Internet are truly awesome, and it is possible to develop and execute your entire investment career without leaving your computer (though we'd urge you to get out now and then and feel the sun; investing should be a means to an end, not an obsession).

This chapter can't attempt to be a guide to online investing, because that subject is far too big to tackle in so few words. In fact, it is a subject that warrants a book all to itself, and . . . as if by magic, here's one we prepared earlier: fortuitously, it's called *The Fool's Guide to Online Investing*, by Nigel Roberts. It covers most of what you will need to get out there on the Web and start investing. What we are doing here is briefly touching on the power of the Internet to help you.

But first a quick look at one thing it's not about.

What it's not about

It would have been close to impossible to go through 1999 without coming across a story about day trading on the Internet and how its ease of access is encouraging more and more people to gamble their future wealth on hot tips and get-rich-quick attempts. Impossible, that is, if you read newspapers or watch television.

And why is it that the tiny minority of day traders is given such high-profile coverage in the press, while the millions of long-term private investors out there are almost completely ignored? It's because shock and scandal sell newspapers and keep eyes glued to the screen, but boring stories of ordinary folk who are doing fine don't have quite the same impact. Can you imagine a news headline saying something like 'Woman Invests In Index Tracker, Makes 12 Per Cent'? No, we can't really see it either.

Day trading, which we talked about back in Chapter Eight, is something that has certainly boomed with the arrival of the Internet, but so has rational long-term investing. A 1999 American survey estimated that there were approximately 15,000 active day traders in the US. But when you compare that with the millions of Americans who invest in shares in some form or other, you might start to wonder about the relative amounts of press coverage that the two groups get.

Information and research

Information. We've met that precious commodity many times throughout this book. Information and the analysis of information are what make the real difference between successful and unsuccessful investors. The Internet provides vast amounts of information for private investors today. At the Motley Fool, for example, we publish company news, company financial snapshots, share prices and charts, amongst other goodies, and provide our discussion boards (many of which are dedicated to individual companies) for readers to swap information and opinion.

Information is no longer the preserve of the professionals.

It's not gospel

Something that we should always be aware of, and wary of, as we explore this great new medium further and further, is that just because something is published on the Internet, it isn't necessarily true.

While it is wonderful to be able to swap opinions about investments and to hold discussions with hundreds of similarly-minded people all over the world, we must always remember that we don't actually know the people we are talking with, and must never make any assumptions about their expertise or their honesty.

It might help to think of the Internet as a big pub, in which anyone can voice any opinion they like. Many of us pick up gossip in such places, and they may be great for spreading local information, but would we treat the words of a stranger the same way we might treat a report in the Financial Times? No, of course we wouldn't. We should treat all such information with caution, and never act on any claims that we can't verify for ourselves.

What we have found with the Motley Fool online community is that a number of regular contributors acquire high reputations through their continued Foolish writing, the value of which has been built up over time. Building an online community is very much the same as building a conventional community; you need to take a little time getting to know people before you can tell who shares your thoughts, who provides the most useful information and feedback, but also, sadly, who talks rubbish and is best avoided.

At the Fool we are constantly working on ways to help our users select and search out the best content. Stop by our discussion boards to see how this works.

The Internet is the perfect medium for research too. In fact, a lot of the research for this book was conducted through the Internet (though a fair bit was also done by good old-fashioned legwork). Want to know about a company? Having checked out its financial snapshot on a site such as the Fool, and having read all the recent news flow about the company, where do you get more in-depth investor information? You may well find an awful lot of what you want on the company's own Web site. Many companies these days, particularly the larger ones, have Investor Information areas on their sites, which provide us with their annual results and interim statements free of charge. Usually we can download them on to our computers and read them at our leisure. Some day, all companies will do the same.

Online dealing

If you are just starting to manage your own personal invest-ments and need to find a stockbroker, the chances are that you will end up using an online service. All the major execution-only brokers have either already shifted the focus of their activities to the Internet or are planning to do so.

Online brokers generally provide the cheapest deals, as they have fewer overheads than traditional bricks and mortar brokerage firms. They also provide services that are pretty easy to use. Just a few clicks with your mouse and you have the current prices of your chosen shares in front of you. Another click or two and the deed is done; you've bought or sold some shares. It's less hassle than talking to a person on the phone (having had to wait ages in a telephone queue first, quite possibly, racking up the phone bill), and much less intimidating than having to walk to a real office and confront some important-looking bloke in a pin-stripe suit.

Financial shopping

Want to buy an index tracker but don't know what different companies offer and what their charges are? Check out their Web sites or some of the sites that aggregate product information, such as Moneyextra (**www.moneyextra.co.uk**). You'll be able to search for comparative information about products and decide who is giving the best deal for your particular needs.

Power

Perhaps the most important thing that the Internet brings to ordinary investors is the power of our combined voices. By enabling thousands of diverse individuals to get together on a common platform, the Internet helps ordinary people to achieve things and to slowly but surely defeat the vested interests that still dominate much of the financial services industry. See the next section, 'The real information revolution', for just one example of this.

The real information revolution

One of the things that we at the Fool really don't like is the practice of selective disclosure. This practice, which many companies indulge in, involves selectively releasing information to analysts and institutional shareholders ahead of releasing the information to the general public (and therefore ahead of ordinary private shareholders like us).

We believe that all such information belongs equally to every single one of a company's shareholders, and that giving some (the big institutional ones) preferential access to it is immoral.

As it happens, over in the USA the Securities and Exchange Commission (the SEC) is proposing a change that would prohibit companies from selectively disclosing information. And the Fool wholeheartedly supports such an initiative.

Wall Street, not surprisingly, doesn't want to take this lying down, and has been lobbying hard to keep things exactly as they are. But the Foolish community in the US has been doing its bit in the battle for freedom of information, and during the public comment period, Fool followers contributed almost half of all the individual responses received by the SEC.

The SEC is considering the proposal further, and we should hear something soon. Thanks to the power that the Internet brings to ordinary people (that's us), the big institutions aren't having it all their own way any more.

We have provided a list of some useful Internet addresses in Appendix C to get you started in the online world.

Teaching your kids about the Internet

Actually, you'll probably find they're going to teach you about the Internet. Ever seen a five-year old handling a computer mouse? They look like they were born with it in their hand. Kids these days are growing up using the Internet in the same way as you or I grew up using the telephone. It's such a natural means of communication that they don't even think about it, and that's the way it should be.

But if you don't need to teach them how to use the Internet, what you can still teach them is how to use it responsibly. There are similar dangers out there to those that, sadly, exist in the physical world. They shouldn't talk to strangers, be enticed into pyramid selling schemes, browse explicit pornography, or search out information about torturing small furry animals. All these things are Bad in the virtual or the physical world.

So, in the same way that you wouldn't let your seven year

old walk into town alone, you shouldn't be letting them surf on their own either. Make sure you supervise access with them until you feel confident they know their way around and know which districts to enter and which to avoid. After that, you may be happy for them to surf on their own, but with the supervision of a software program which you can set to block some kinds of unsavoury sites. However, to be honest, it's probably better to give them a reliable sense of what's good and what's bad, rather than relying on blocking things.

Don't let security concerns put you off, though. The opportunity the Internet offers your child to learn about the world, communicate with others and get to grips with taking control of their own life is priceless. If you can help them learn how to make best use of it at an early age, you'll have given them a precious gift indeed.

Chapter Fifteen: To finish

This is not the end. It is not even the beginning of the end. But it is, perhaps, the end of the beginning.
Winston Churchill

What? We're finished? No, actually, not at all. We may be getting to the end of the book, but we hope that you are just at the start of a long and fruitful investing life for your precious children. If we have helped you to think about the financial security that could so easily lie ahead for them and we have in any way inspired you to start a regular investment programme on their behalf, even if it's just to go and do some more research, then this book will have served its purpose.

No book, especially one of this modest size, can hope to teach you all you need to know about investing. In particular, we haven't tried to teach you in detail about how to analyze companies, the different ways there are to evaluate a possible investment, or what individual strategies you might like to consider when choosing investments for yourself. But we hope we have given you a taster for the kind of things that are available to you if you want them.

And if you decide that an index tracker fund is all you need for your children, then you will still be doing them proud. By putting regular savings into one of these over a long period (and educating your children about money so that they will want to take over and continue it when they are earning for themselves), you will get an annual return that is just a shade short of your chosen stock market index itself (after allowing for charges and errors in tracking the index). If that chosen index is the FTSE 100, you will be putting your children's financial future in the hands of the UK's 100 biggest companies, many of whom are world leaders on a truly global scale. We reckon those are pretty safe hands.

And you know what else? Buying an index tracker will require no research beyond choosing one with suitable minimum monthly contributions, low charges, and a decently low tracking error (all of which they should be able to tell you in an instant). After that, you will have to spend precisely zero time each year analyzing your investments, no time at all watching out for company news and performance figures, and not one second on the phone to your broker buying and selling shares. And that total absence of future effort will, if the past is anything to go by, get you a return that beats more than 90 per cent of the professionals.

If you want to do better than an index tracker and fancy selecting your own companies (or you want to get that tracker going and add to it with a few share selections of your own, as many people choose to do), then good for you. If you can get together with a few like-minded individuals (or with many thousands of them on the Motley Fool site), then you will probably find that instead of the time-consuming and difficult chore that investing is often made out to be, it becomes a stimulating and rewarding pastime. Hopefully, it will become so for your children too.

The Motley Fool has a selection of other books that should help you to go further, and they are listed in Appendix C. But if you really want to start doing your own research and choosing your kids' investments for yourself, then you have to get online. You'll be left behind if you don't.

We look forward to seeing you over on the Motley Fool Web site, and we'd love to hear how you get on over the years, and to share in your experiences.

See you soon.

Appendix A – Compound it!

*'Reeling and Writhing, of course, to begin with, the Mock Turtle
replied: and then the different branches of Arithmetic –
Ambition, Distraction, Uglification, and Derision.'*
Lewis Carroll

We've seen the magic of compound returns in Chapter Three, and good magicians never reveal the secrets of their magic. But we're not very good magicians. And it's really quite easy magic. None of this appendix is actually necessary for learning about investing, but we are including it here to help those people who find it hard to believe just how much all this compounding can add up to. It can be a bit mind-boggling, after all, but if you know how it's worked out, you can verify it for yourself.

Now, before you groan and mutter, 'Oh, no, it's like being at school all over again,' listen here. . . it's *educational*, see? And educating your kids is as much a part of turning them into millionaires as saving money for them in the first place. And we promise it's all going to be logical and we'll take it step by step. The hardest bits of arithmetic that we assume you can do are multiplication and division. Anything else will be explained as we go along. And to be honest, you won't even have to do multiplication or division unless you're determined to work things out with a calculator and a pencil. If you can handle a computer and a spreadsheet program (such as Microsoft Excel), and you're happy entering formulae into cells, then that's all you really need.

But if you aren't interested in the nitty-gritty of how to

calculate the value of compound returns, or you just don't feel comfortable doing sums, then that's fine. You can cheerily skip this appendix and read the rest of the book with no problems at all. You'll be able to handle your investments without it. Also, if you are one of the millions of people who have never used a spreadsheet (and that applies to the majority of people over school age, we'd guess), then perhaps you should just skip this appendix too.

But one thought: if your children are old enough to handle some arithmetic, you might be doing them a fair bit of good by putting this in front of them (after they've read Chapter Three and wondered at the riches that will surely await them if they invest prudently, of course). And while you're at it, giving them the whole book to read might do them some good too. If you're still with us at this point, then bully for you - we're glad you've decided to give it a go.

The Wonder Of Spreadsheets

Back when a lot of us were learning maths at school, we didn't have computers (in fact, a lot of us are old enough not to have even had calculators), and calculating things like compound interest was tedious. But that's all changed now, and things are a lot easier.

The examples in this book were all done using an Apple Macintosh computer and a copy of Microsoft Excel 98. Excel for Windows is pretty much identical, so you can follow exactly the same process if you use a Windows computer. Excel provides a jolly useful little function for calculating the future value of an investment if it's made in the form of regular identical contributions (and it can handle a lump sum as a starter too).

All you need to do is open up a new spreadsheet and use the 'FV' function ('Future Value', geddit, though it might be called something else if you are using a different spreadsheet; and the parameters are almost certain to be different, so you'll need to check your help documentation), and enter something like this into a cell. . .

= FV((1+0.06)^(1/12)−1, 60*12, −(25), 0, 1)

Cool, eh? This, by the way, is the calculation that gave us the result of little Fred's 60 years of 6 per cent per year savings from Chapter 1.2, and if it looks a little daunting, please bear with us while we attempt to explain it step by step.

What do all those numbers mean? Every function that Excel supports is described in the online help that comes with it (you did install the Help files when you installed Excel, didn't you? What, you didn't? Well, you'd better go and dig out that Excel CD then).

Looking up the Excel Help for the FV function shows the parameters (that's the numbers inside the parentheses after the 'FV', separated by commas). They will be something like this. . .

= FV(Rate, Periods, Payment, Lump, Type)

Actually, we've given the parameters slightly different names here, because the Excel Help uses names that are a little cryptic and less intuitive. And Microsoft's explanations of those parameters are perhaps slightly more abstract than we really need for handling our compound return calculation, so we'll use a simpler Foolish description of them instead. But before we do that, bear in mind that our regular payments are going in monthly and so we need to use monthly periods and a monthly rate of return too.

Rate = Percentage return per period

Periods = The number of periods

Payment = The payment made each period

Lump = The size of any lump sum we start with as an initial investment

Type = When the payments are made

Now, let's examine the values we have actually used for calculating Fred's 60-year fortune. The first parameter is the rate of return. We know that Fred is achieving 6 per cent per year, and the calculation shown, $(1+0.06)^{(1/12)}−1$, is how we calculate the monthly equivalent. If you are happy to use that formula for deriving the monthly rate of return, then you can just go ahead and not worry about it. And that's probably the best thing to do for now because we are, after all, talking about the *easy* way here. But we'll come back to it when we consider the *hard* way a little later (which you can, of course, skip if you want). Oh, and the '^' just means 'to the power of', such that '2^5', for example, would mean 'two to the power of five.' But what does 'to the power of' really mean anyway? If it doesn't mean much to you at the moment, the section below, 'A Power of Good', will explain all.

Next comes the period, which is the total number of payment periods over the life of the investment. As we are investing every month for 60 years, that's 60*12 (or 720) periods.

The payment made each period is easy, that's £25.

The initial lump sum investment is easy too. There isn't one, so it's a big fat zero.

The last parameter, the type, allows you to specify when the payments are made. You can choose to make your periodic payments at either the beginning of each period by specifying this as 1, or at the end of each period by specifying 0. We use the beginning method throughout, as that is the more usual way of thinking of investments. (We tend to think of it as saving some money, and then seeing what return we get every subsequent month after the investment.)

A Power of Good

You've never found the need to raise 2 to the power of 5 before? Don't worry, you're in good company; most of the world's population has never done it either. So we'll explain.

Two to the power of two means 2*2, which equals 4.
Two to the power of three means 2*2*2, which equals 8.
Two to the power of 19 means 2*2*2*. . . all the way up to 19.

But anyway, what's the result of the calculation? If you've entered the formula correctly, you should get that answer of £165,090.18, to the nearest penny.

Top of the class, then, if that's the result you got.

There is one thing you might have noticed if you were looking carefully though, and it's to do with two of the parameters – payment (the periodic payment) and lump (the initial lump sum). Did you spot it? If you look closely you'll see there's a wee minus sign in the payment parameter. Yep, that's what Excel requires; your investment contributions need to be entered as negative numbers. It's just part of a convention for expressing financial calculations.

That's how to work out the future value of a periodic investment, but how do you use the formula to calculate the future value of a single lump sum investment instead? What do you do if Fred's parents, instead of setting him off along the path of investing £25 per month for 60 years, just invest a single sum of £2,000 and leave it at that? What is that going to be worth after 60 years?

Again, that's not too difficult (you just knew we were going to say that, didn't you?). Use the FV function again, but instead of that '–25' that you entered last time as the monthly investment amount, just enter nought. And instead of the zero you entered for the initial lump sum, stick in that juicy 2,000 (not forgetting the quirky minus sign, of course). The formula for calculating Fred's new fortune is now. . .

=FV(0.06, 60, 0, –2000, 1)

Notice that we don't bother breaking it down into months this time, and instead we just use yearly periods, 60 of them in fact, and the annual rate of return. That's simply because, as there are no monthly payments, we don't need to bother with months at all.

Oh, and the answer is £65,975.38.

Hmm, young Fred would have been much better off with that £25 per month, wouldn't he? But supposing that Fred's parents had that spare £2,000, and were still able to invest a further £25 per month. What would that amount to? You could, of course, just do the two parts separately and add them together, which would be perfectly satisfactory. But you can do it in one step, and yes, you're ahead of us aren't you? You enter both the periodic £25 and the initial £2,000 at the same time, thus. . .

=FV((1+0.06)^(1/12) –1, 60*12, –25, –2000, 1)

And yes, because we are now making monthly payments again, we have to go back to the monthly version of the formula.

And the answer is £231,065.56.

Which just happens to be £165,090.18 plus £65,975.38.

Handling Multiple Payment Periods

The examples of compounding that we have worked with in this book are actually a little unrealistic in some ways. In particular, it is pretty unlikely that someone will invest exactly the same monthly amount over their entire working life. Instead, as inflation and earnings increase, regular savers are far more likely to increase their savings in line with their income and expenditure. So we might expect to see an investment pattern something like £200 per month for a couple of years, then £220 per month for a few more years, and so on. Or during times of temporary increase in expenditure (when children or grandchildren arrive, for example), we might expect to see regular investments being cut back.

So when working out the expected value of your long-term investments, you'll need to cope with different amounts of money over different periods. Spreadsheets don't tend to offer a single function that will handle that kind of thing, so the way to do it is to simply calculate each period separately and add them all together.

Working Backwards

One final thing that you might find useful is being able to work backwards from an expected final value and work out what annual percentage rate of return it represents. Have you ever seen adverts for investments that quote possible final values, but that do not quote a rate of return? That's probably because the rate of return is rather low.

Using a spreadsheet, this calculation is also quite easy. Most spreadsheets provide a function, and the one provided by Excel is as follows. . .

= RATE(Periods, Payment, Lump, Final Value, Type, Guess)

Periods = The number of periods

Payment = The payment made each period

Lump = The size of any lump sum we start with as an initial investment

Final Value = The expected final value of the investment

Type = When the payments are made (1 = start of each period)

Guess = an estimate to help it on its way (the calculation is done by an iterative process and your estimate might help, though it can usually be omitted).

Here's an example. Starting with the final value of our 60-year investment of £25 per month at 6 per cent, which comes in at £165,090.18, and omitting the Guess parameter we get. . .

= RATE(60*12, 25, 0, –165,090.18, 1)

And that gives us a monthly rate of return of 0.00486755, which is almost 0.49 per cent. To get an annual rate, we need the twelfth power. . .

Annual Rate = $((1+0.00486755)^{12})$ −1

Annual Rate = 0.06, or 6%

You might like to work backwards from the other examples we have looked at and deduce their rates of return. Or you might not, which is probably a lot more sensible. Either way, if you use the RATE function with any lump sums, the lump sum itself must be entered as positive, not negative, and the expected final value negative. (Quirky, yes, but that's life).

Appendix B – Jargon unravelled

'When I use a word,' Humpty Dumpty said, in rather a scornful tone, 'it means just what I choose it to mean; neither more nor less.'

Lewis Carroll

Analyst: A financial professional who analyzes companies in order to estimate a valuation. Analysts are frequently paid by the number of opaque recommendations that they issue, and which Fools usually ignore.

Annual report: A yearly statement of a public company's operating and financial performance, often punctuated by pictures of families enjoying the firm's products and/or services. A very important document for any analysis of a potential investment nevertheless.

Annuity: The investment you purchase with your pension fund, which will provide you with a regular income in your retirement. Because it is aimed at providing you with income, the majority of the fund is invested in bonds and government securities. The annuity seller has to guess how long you will you live and pays you an income accordingly. When you die the money stays with the annuity seller. Should you die very shortly after purchasing the annuity, this leads to a situation colloquially known as a 'bummer'. The law currently requires you to purchase an annuity with your pension fund by the time you are 75.

Bare trust: A simple mechanism for investing in the name of a child but retaining the power of control over the investment until the child is 18 (or 16 in Scotland). Chapter Nine covers bare trusts in some detail.

Bear: 1) A cuddly toy popular with young (and not so young) children; 2) an investor with a pessimistic outlook, and who expects share prices to fall. Fools investing long term for their children will probably gain more benefit from the former than the latter. See also: *Bull*.

Beat The Footsie: A mechanical investment strategy based on selecting companies by their *Dividend Yield*. See Chapter Eight.

Beta: 1) The second letter of the Greek alphabet; 2) a term used by *chartists* to refer to the short-term *volatility* of a share price. Neither is likely to be of any real interest to long-term investors.

Bid: The price at which you can sell a share

Bid-offer spread: See *Spread*.

Blue chip: A share in a large, prestigious company. British Telecommunications is a blue chip company, as is HSBC. Many of the shares making up the FTSE 100 are blue chips.

Bonds: Bonds represent loans to companies or governments. If you buy a bond, you are lending money to the issuer, and you will usually collect some regular interest payments until your money is eventually returned to you. Government-issued *gilts* are a type of bond. Not a good choice when investing long term for your children, as Chapter Four illustrates

Broker: Someone who acts as an agent for buying or selling something; in the Foolish investment world, usually referring to a s*tockbroker*.

BTF: See *Beat The Footsie*.

Bull: An investor with an optimistic outlook, and who expects share prices to rise. Fools are long-term bulls. And short term? We can't predict that reliably. See also: *Bear*.

Capital gain: The profit you make when you sell shares (or other assets) at a higher price than you paid for them. Capital Gains Tax may be due on such a profit.

Carpetbagging: The practice of depositing minimal amounts of money in *mutual* building society accounts, or buying minimal insurance policies from *mutual* insurance companies, in the hope of landing a fat windfall if the company *demutualizes*.

Chartist: A person who appears to believe that everything that there is to be learned about an investment in a public company can be deduced from a chart of the company's short-term share price movements.

CAT: Standing for 'Charges, Access, Terms', the CAT mark is awarded to investment products that satisfy what the government feels is reasonable in all three categories.

Child: A heavily *front-loaded* investment, but one that can reap impressive long-term returns if nurtured well.

Commission: The charge levied by your broker when you buy or sell shares. Excessive commissions caused by too frequent trading is a common killer of long-term profits.

Compounding: The jewel in the long-term investor's crown; the thing that would have made £100 invested in the stock market in 1869 worth £20 million today. Chapters Three and Four explain.

Cyberspace: The electronic world in which the Internet exists. To many, a land of free speech and freedom of information that enhances the empowerment of individuals. To others, an imaginary world inhabited by spotty adolescent *geeks* who can't handle normal human relationships.

Day trader: A person who stakes all on the ability to out-guess the stock market on a minute-by-minute, hour-by-hour, day-by-day basis; a *stockbroker*'s best friend; a loser. See Chapter Eight.

Demutualize: To surrender a company's *mutual* status by converting it into a publicly-owned company and distributing shares amongst the company's customers or other stakeholders.

Discount broker, or **Execution-only broker:** A *stockbroker* who only offers the service of buying and selling shares, and who offers no advice or investment management services. Perfect for the long-distance Fool.

Diversification: The act of spreading your investments over a number of different companies and possibly different sectors to protect yourself from a bad performance from any individual one of them. See Chapter Eight.

Dividend: A payment to shareholders that normally represents a portion of a company's profits. Occasionally, special dividends may be paid for other purposes.

Dividend yield: A company's dividend divided by the current share price, expressed as a percentage. Different companies have different policies on the size of their dividend payouts.

Dow Jones Industrial Average: The 30 companies chosen by editors of Dow Jones & Company that are supposed to epitomize the very best American corporations and reflect the landscape of corporate America, although high-tech companies are somewhat underrepresented.

Earnings Per Share (EPS): A measure of the amount of a company's earnings that is attributable to each share in existence. It is calculated by dividing the company's total net earnings by the total number of shares.

EPIC: The short code allocated to a company by the London Stock Exchange which can be used to clearly identify that company. British Telecommunications, for example, has the EPIC 'BT.A', and Barclays Bank uses 'BARC'.

Equities: Another word for shares.

Execution-only broker: See *Discount Broker*.

Financial adviser: See *Tied Financial Adviser* and *Independent Financial Adviser*.

Financial services industry: 1) A remarkably affluent industrial sector, mostly out to service itself by using slick sales techniques and misleading literature to separate the general public from its savings; or 2) a body of companies relentlessly dedicated to providing value in financial services to its customers. You decide.

Fool: Fools are investors who have learned enough about investing to take charge of their own financial futures, tossing aside the Wise advisers and fund managers whose aim is to enrich themselves, not their clients. See *Motley Fool*.

Front load: A front-loaded investment is one that carries up-front charges. Any regular investment that levies a charge on each contribution, for example, is a front-loaded investment. The worst type of front loading in recent years has been by endowment companies that take the first year or two of contributions and keep them for themselves in charges.

FTSE 100: An *index* containing the 100 largest companies by *market capitalization* on the London Stock Exchange.

FTSE 250: An *index* containing the next 250 largest companies, after the FTSE 100, by *market capitalization* on the London Stock Exchange.

FTSE All Share Index: An *index* containing the 900 or so companies quoted on the London Stock Exchange's main list. Like the FTSE 100 and FTSE 250, the index is named after the *Financial Times* (FT) and the London Stock Exchange (SE), who are its joint owners. The FTSE-ASI and the FTSE 100 are the indices generally tracked by index trackers.

Full-service stockbroker: A *stockbroker* who takes full control of your investments, and who thinks he knows what is best for you. See Chapter Seven.

Geek: A term (originally derogatory) applied to computer hackers, software gurus, and assorted net-heads. The term 'geek' is a badge often worn with pride these days, particularly by people who have forgotten what the sun looks like.

Gilts: When the government needs to borrow money, it sells you these. See *bonds*.

IFA: See *Independent Financial Adviser*.

Independent financial adviser: A salesperson. Usually one who attempts to sell you the financial products that will pay him the highest rates of commission rather than the ones that will provide you with the best returns. The 'independent' bit means he can sell you products from a range of suppliers rather than being restricted to a single supplier. Rarely, but more Foolishly, the term can encompass individuals who charge by the hour, gain no benefit from high commissions, and therefore face no conflict of interest when it comes to your investments.

Index: A figure calculated from the share prices of a specific set of companies, and used for measuring stock market performance. The *FTSE 100*, for example, is calculated from the share prices of the UK's 100 biggest companies by *market capitalization*. See Chapter Eight.

Index tracker: An investment fund that simply spreads its money across the constituents of a stock market *index*. Cheap to administer, index trackers closely follow their chosen indices and carry low charges. Index trackers typically outperform more than 90 per cent of *managed funds*. See Chapter Eight.

Institutions: Institutional investors include pension funds, unit trusts and insurance companies. These are the big players in the stock market as they have a lot of money to invest, and as major shareholders they often have a say in company decisions.

Internet: Ooh, you really didn't pay much attention to the 20th century, did you? See Chapter Fourteen.

Investment club: A group of investors who pool their money and meet regularly to discuss which shares to buy and sell. See Chapter Twelve for an impressive example.

ISA: Individual Savings Account. An investment wrapper designed to encourage long-term investing and which has significant tax breaks attached. In fact, all income and capital gains within an ISA are tax free. Children, though, can't have them.

Managed fund: An investment fund that employs expensive managers in the belief that they possess superior share selection skills and can thus perform better than the stock market average. More than 90 per cent of UK managed funds have so far failed to match the stock market's average performance. See Chapter Seven for more on fund managers.

Margin trading: A predominately American phenomenon, margin trading is the practice of borrowing money from a stockbroker to invest, and only having to provide a minimum percentage of the value of the shares, the margin, in cash. Not Foolish, and very dangerous.

Market capitalization: The total market value of a company. Market capitalization is calculated by multiplying a company's share price by the number of shares in existence.

Market makers: The 'wholesalers' who actually make the market for the shares in companies that investors wish to buy and sell, and with whom *stockbrokers* deal. With an obligation to trade in their chosen shares, it is market makers who set the *spread* and who profit from the difference between the *bid* and *offer* prices.

Mid-price: The figure usually quoted for share prices. The prices in newspapers, on BBC Teletext, and in many other places are mid-prices. The mid-price is usually around half-way between the *bid* and *offer* prices, and is intended as a general guideline.

Motley Fool: What? You've read this far and you still don't know what the Motley Fool is? The Motley Fool is dedicated to teaching people how to successfully manage their own investments for themselves. Our mission? To educate, amuse, and enrich. Check out the Foreword for more shameless self-promotion.

Mutual: A term mainly applied to building societies and insurance companies that have no shareholders, and which are owned by their savers and borrowers. A dying breed, with their conversion to banks being responsible for the popular new sport of *carpetbagging*.

National Curriculum: A set of guidelines for schools, enabling them to improve their relative rankings by increasing the number of exam passes that they achieve.

Offer: The price at which you can buy a share.

Online investing: The same as conventional investing, except using the extraordinary resources of the *Internet* to help you out.

P/E ratio (price-to-earnings): A share's price divided by its annual *earnings per share*. The P/E ratio gives some idea of how a company is valued in relation to its earnings.

Penny shares: Penny shares are low-priced shares, frequently trading for just a few pennies. They usually have high *spreads*, which means that a high return is needed to break even. Companies with shares priced in pennies are often very small too, and their prices can sometimes be manipulated by dishonest means. All in all, not a recommended investment for Fools.

Portfolio: A collection of investments. For example, your investment portfolio might be made up of shares in a dozen different companies. Or it might have some bonds, some shares, and other investments.

Real world, the: A delusion caused by insufficient exposure to *cyberspace*.

Relative strength: A measure of a company's share price performance. Companies with high relative strength have seen their share prices rise higher than those with lower relative strength.

Share: Part-ownership of a company; it's as simple as that.

Shareholder: You, Fool! If you own shares in a company you get an invitation to the company's annual general meeting (the AGM), receive copies of financial reports, and you have the right to vote on the members of the Board of Directors and other company matters.

Spread: The difference between the *bid* and *offer* prices of a share.

Stock: An American term for shares (strictly, 'shares in common stock'). The two terms tend to be used interchangeably.

Stockbroker: Woody Allen described a stockbroker as someone who invests your money until it has all gone. Normally it is a middleman who buys and sells shares on your behalf and who earns commission on the transactions. Considered by many to be the fifth-oldest profession after prostitutes, pimps, tax collectors and accountants.

Tied financial adviser: A financial adviser who is even less independent than an *Independent Financial Adviser*. These are company salespeople, trying to sell you the products of the company they work for. Buying investment products from them is not a recommended activity for Fools.

Underperformance: What more than 90 per cent of the UK's active fund managers excel at. See Chapter Seven.

URL: Uniform Resource Locator. There, that sounds impressive, doesn't it? It's just the geeky name for a Web address, like **www.fool.co.uk** for example. Sometimes referred to as a 'Universal Resource Locator'.

Volatility: The degree by which a share price tends to move. The more the price moves up and down, the more volatile the share. Volatility tends to even out over the long term.

Wise: The financial services industry, which has served us so badly for so long. If they're 'Wise', being 'Foolish' seems like a much better long-term bet.

Appendix C – References

Other books

As modestly as we possibly can, we'd like to suggest that the following Fool books might be useful sources of further information. . .

The Motley Fool UK Investment Guide, by David Berger with David and Tom Gardner, takes a more detailed look at long-term investing, but in a light-hearted and easy-to-read style.

The Motley Fool UK Investment Workbook, by David Berger and Bruce Jackson, takes a practical approach to learning about investment, and uses step-by-step exercises to show how to go about it.

The Fool's Guide to Investment Clubs, by Mark Goodson, tells you all about, er, investment clubs. If you were impressed by the achievements of Sunderland High School and would like to learn how to set up a club, Mark's extensive experience should be a help.

The Fool's Guide to Online Investing, by Nigel Roberts, provides all you need to know to make the most of the most important research tool that investors have at their disposal, the Internet.

How To Invest When You Don't Have Any Money: The Fool's Guide, by Christopher Spink, might be just the thing for hard-pressed parents who don't feel they've got anything to spare.

All of the above Fool books are published by Boxtree and can be bought online from the Fool Bookshop at **www.amazon.co.uk/exec/obidos/subst/third-party/motley/motley.html/**

The ProShare Guide to Investment Clubs is a very useful

publication for anyone actually wanting to set up an investment club. Most clubs, in fact, consider it an essential. It can be ordered from the ProShare Web site at **www.proshare.org**.

Useful places on the Web

The Motley Fool. . .

The Motley Fool UK Site (**www.fool.co.uk**) is really the core of the UK Foolish world. Registration is free, so please come and share in what the Fool community has to offer.

The Motley Fool US Site (**www.fool.com**) is the site that started it all. It's a fair bit bigger than the UK site, and is focused on the USA of course. You may find it educational. We also have Fool Germany (**www.fool.de**), but you need to understand German for that one.

The Motley Fool discussion boards (**boards.fool.co.uk/**) are the heart of the Fool community, with boards available for all sorts of investment-related topics, including many individual company message boards.

The Investing For Children board, which can be found in the 'Managing Your Finances' folder, is the one on which eager parents can share their ideas and experiences.

The Index Tracker board, which is also in the 'Managing Your Finances' folder, is the place where you'll find plenty of information and opinions about index tracker suppliers.

Useful informational sites. . .

The Credit Suisse First Boston Equity-Gilt Study (**www.csfb. com/eqres/eqres_gilt.html**) shows how shares have performed since 1869, and can be accessed free.

The Barclays Capital Equity-Gilt Study (**www.barcap.com/ egs/**) does the same thing, but starting in 1899. It's not free though, you have to pay if you want the details.

The WM Company active versus passive fund comparison (www.index-tracking.co.uk) shows just how true it is that past performance is no guide to future performance when it comes to actively managed investment funds.

For a site that lists who offers what in the way of index trackers and other unit trusts, mortgages, insurance and more, MoneyExtra (www.moneyextra) is hard to beat.

The Inland Revenue site (www.inlandrevenue.gov.uk) is well organized, offers plenty of information and has many informational leaflets for downloading. The Inland Revenue also provides a telephone helpline on 0845 9800645.

ProShare (www.proshare.org/) is best known for its help with investment clubs, but you'll also find details of ProShare's National Investment Programme for Schools and Colleges.

Warren Buffett's letters to shareholders of Berkshire Hathaway (www.berkshirehathaway.com/) are legendary and provide a wealth of investment pearls.

For all kinds of statistics about the UK, the UK Government Statistics site (www.statistics.gov.uk/stats/ukinfigs/ukinfig.htm) has plenty to pore over.

Other useful (or fun) sites. . .

Google (www.google.com) provides an extremely effective search site that is rapidly becoming a favourite with many Web users.

Cawley's Latin Dictionary and Grammar Aid (www.nd.edu/~archives/latgramm.htm) is very handy for making up bogus Latin names.

The Irresponsible Internet Statistics Generator (www.anamorph.com/docs/stats/stats.html) does, well, exactly what it says.